CULTURE

Books by Michael H. Agar

Angel Dust: An Ethnographic Study of PCP Users (coeditor)
Dope Double Agent: The Naked Emperor on Drugs
Independents Declared: The Dilemmas of Independent Trucking
Language Shock: Understanding the Culture of Conversation
The Lively Science: Remodeling Human Social Research
The Professional Stranger: An Informal Introduction to Ethnography
Ripping and Running: A Formal Ethnography of Urban Heroin Addicts
Speaking of Ethnography

CULTURE

How to Make It Work
in a World of Hybrids

MICHAEL H. AGAR

ROWMAN & LITTLEFIELD
Lanham • Boulder • New York • London

Executive Editor: Nancy Roberts
Assistant Editor: Megan Manzano
Senior Marketing Manager: Amy Whitaker

Credits and acknowledgments for material borrowed from other sources, and reproduced with permission, appear on the appropriate page within the text.

Published by Rowman & Littlefield
An imprint of The Rowman & Littlefield Publishing Group, Inc.
4501 Forbes Boulevard, Suite 200, Lanham, Maryland 20706
www.rowman.com

6 Tinworth Street, London SE11 4AL, United Kingdom

British Library Cataloguing in Publication Information Available

Library of Congress Cataloging-in-Publication Data
Names: Agar, Michael, author.
Title: Culture : how to make it work in a world of hybrids / Michael H. Agar.
Description: Lanham, Maryland : Rowman & Littlefield, [2019] | Includes
    bibliographical references and index.
Identifiers: LCCN 2018035259 (print) | LCCN 2018046231 (ebook) | ISBN
    9781538118122 (electronic) | ISBN 9781538118108 (cloth : alk. paper) |
    ISBN 9781538118115 (pbk. : alk. paper)
Subjects: LCSH: Culture.
Classification: LCC GN357 (ebook) | LCC GN357 .A43 2019 (print) | DDC
    306—dc23
LC record available at https://lccn.loc.gov/2018035259

♾️™ The paper used in this publication meets the minimum requirements of American National Standard for Information Sciences—Permanence of Paper for Printed Library Materials, ANSI/NISO Z39.48-1992.

Printed in the United States of America

CONTENTS

Foreword

"RECENTLY THE TIME HORIZON became visible." This is how Mike opens *Culture: How to Make It Work in a World of Hybrids*, and I knew that twenty years of our conversation regarding culture was coming to a close.

This book is a bittersweet irony for me. In the spring of 2017, Mike let me know that the draft was done, if I had time to look at it. I printed off a copy and started reading it after long days at work, in between running my sons to baseball practices and dance lessons. In one of my last email exchanges with Mike, I wrote about some of my impressions from the first chapter, not having gotten very far into the book. I told him the ideas were powerful to me, particularly foregrounding Culture as something shared by all of humanity rather than culture as a set of beliefs and values that can divide and separate us. After I signed off, I said, "P.S. Glad you are finally answering my question: what is culture? ;)" He quickly shot an email back: "Good lord, maybe I wrote the thing to finally answer your question about culture."

Two decades ago, Mike graciously agreed to meet with me at a coffee shop. I wanted to pick his brain on discourse analysis for a grad school paper I was writing. The conversation eventually turned to culture. I was struggling with the term as a grad student in anthropology. I was teetering on the edge of throwing the concept out the window even though the discipline I was courting had invented the term. It has been coopted by so many to the point that I wasn't sure it held any meaning. While I knew that my own values and beliefs were coded with culture, I had no idea what words to use to define my "culture." Mike humored me and took me seriously. We engaged in a long email exchange, a printed copy of which I keep in my filing cabinet to this day. But, if I'm truly honest, I never felt settled with the term until I read this book.

And yet I'm not sure that resolving the issue of culture was Mike's point of writing this book; he wanted to make sense of that contested term with an eye toward getting us to think differently about human interactions—from the beginning of time—and suggest a few possibilities that might help us live a little more successfully on this planet. To quote Mike (who was quoting a bumper sticker), "whirled peas." However, I also struggle with putting my own interpretation on Mike's words, because, from my past experiences reading his books, I will understand *Culture* in a whole new way the next time I read it—and each person who reads this book will bring their own experiences and perspectives to it. That is the power of Mike's writing. He writes in a way that is easily accessible, but the theoretical implications run deep and wide, pushing us to expand our thinking from where we are in our own time and place.

Rather than interpreting Mike's words with a guide to *Culture* that I can only write through my own lens, I'm simply going to tell you about some of the concepts that struck me as I read it. My hope is that you will read Mike's words first.

As you probably guessed, Culture is first—not culture with a lowercase *c* (the values and beliefs that bind a group of people together with a common way of seeing the world) but Culture with a capital *C*. Mike reminds us that Culture with a capital *C* is the evolutionary trajectory of humankind, or, as Klein and Edgar called it, the "Culture Big Bang." He tells this story in an engaging way that forced me to think about the transformative role of Culture at the beginning of our human story—at least the one that started some fifty thousand years ago—and how it continues to this day.

From Culture with a capital *C*, our hunting-gathering bands of ancestors formed cultures with a small *c*, each creating their own histories and their own ways of doing things. Culture with a small *c* harnessed the new human abilities of generativity to do things differently, and it employed social constraints to keep all that innovation in control—generativity and constraint were dual forces in the Big Bang.

The focus of anthropology has traditionally been on those small-*c* cultures. But now that we live in a global society where we are all mixes of a variety of influences, describing a "culture" is no longer very useful—or even possible—in understanding someone or resolving differences when we try to work together. We are pretty much all hybrids—multiple "cultures" snake and weave themselves through you and me, people living in a globalized, diverse, interconnected world. And yet culture is still largely seen as the problem that we try to solve with "diversity training" or efforts at "intercultural communication." However, since we are all hybrids in an interconnected world, as Mike proposes, resolving "cultural" differences with "culture" no longer works. So what might?

At the close of chapter 1, Mike writes, "If at least two people share a way of doing at least one task together, a way that could in principle be changed, then we could say that those two people share a *'culture'* for doing that task" (emphasis mine). By defining culture in this way, Mike situates us in the here and now—two or more people engaged in a task and the tacit knowledge that allows them to work together to accomplish it. Mike grounds his concepts in the basics of everyday life: people trying to get something done together.

In his book *Language Shock* (1994), Mike introduced the concept of *languaculture*, which appears again in this book. This linguistic combo is a reminder that culture cannot be separated from language, and vice versa. As he wrote in *Language Shock*, "What I want to happen, what I want you to remember at the end of this book, is that whenever you hear the word *language* or the word *culture*, you might wonder about the missing half" (p. 60). However, this book is rooted in evolutionary theory, and just as big-*C* Culture is part of our rapid evolutionary trajectory, so, too, are the descent of the larynx and the development of a neocortical-vocal tract allowing humans to produce language. It wasn't just the Culture Big Bang that sent us on our *Homo sapiens* trajectory but also the "Languaculture Big Bang." Generativity skyrocketed with language. And anyone who has taken a basic intro course to linguistics knows that constraints are also part and parcel of language, bringing us again to the dual concepts of generativity and constraint. Mike returns to Linguistics 101 to teach us the levels of language: phonology, morphology, syntax, semantics, and pragmatics. This short section on the generativity and constraints of languaculture is, in itself, worth the price of the book. By thinking about this pair through the lens of linguistic labels, Mike expanded my thinking about their importance in our human trajectory in a way that simply thinking about it through the lens of culture never had.

Language and culture to languaculture. Generativity and constraint. A new world of hybrids. These were the concepts that brought me through the first half of Mike's book—and, really, to the world we live in today.

I want to leave you with one more idea from this book: social perspective taking. If we no longer live in a world of bounded little-*c* cultures, but rather in a world where everyone is a hybrid of multiple influences, how do we successfully move forward? Mike's hypothesis incorporates a social perspective taking approach, including empathy (or theory of mind) and ethnographic-like learning-testing-learning, as well as recognizing our very human tendencies toward naïve realism (i.e., thinking that we, and only we, objectively see the world and other people). At the opening of chapter 6, Mike tells the story of doing a workshop for the Army Institute in the beginnings of the Afghan conflict. My sense is that Mike's point in doing the workshop was to convince the attendees—and the United States Army—that there is no cookie-cutter approach to learning "Afghan culture" and that you can't teach your soldiers all they need to know about Afghanistan before they interact with its citizens. Instead, the goal should be to "teach what to do once you get there to learn what you need to know [because] *most of what you learn will happen after you arrive*" (emphasis original) (chapter 6).

Mike presents many examples of successes of social perspective taking in a variety of situations, and he expresses his hope that this book will inspire "some support or time or both" toward further exploring the possibilities of social perspective taking—additional research to examine the failures as well as the successes of the approach, its staying power over time, and whether and under what circumstances the results can diffuse more broadly (chapter 7).

Culture, languaculture, generativity and constraint, a world of hybrids, and social perspective taking are the concepts that kept me thinking long after I set this book down. However, there are many, many more drawn from a wide range of disciplines. In my first reading of *Culture*, these were not what stayed with me, but, given my biographical engagement with Mike and culture, that is not surprising. I trust that your own readings of *Culture* will leave you pondering other concepts—and most definitely walking away with different interpretations of those that struck me. I hope that, using the latest technological innovations, you will reach out to me so we can share a cultural, a hybrid, a universal moment.

I must admit that I often shy away from the idea of human universals. Mike wanted us to recognize human universals as front and center. Culture as that which makes us humans is a human universal; language is a human universal; empathy is a human universal. In the end, it is in "go[ing] directly to human universals, where a connection across hybrids can always be made" (chapter 7).

Finally, what Mike seemed most proud of was that he wrote a transdisciplinary book. Mike's roots in linguistic anthropology serve as the foundation, but he expertly weaves in multiple social sciences, evolution-

ary theory, cognitive science, complexity theory, computer science, organizational theory, social psychology, network theory, and the list goes on.
Putting universals front and center requires transdisciplinary engagement.
And, once again, Mike grounds us with a task. He pushes us to envision
a postdisciplinary age when a student can choose a problem she wants
to work on, work with people all over the disciplinary map, and learn a
whole lot of social perspective taking along the way.

As I write this, in a week it will be May 7. On May 7, 1945, Michael
Henry Agar was born to an Irish-Catholic family living in Chicago, and
Germany surrendered to the Allies. Mike was proud of that biographical
fact. On May 20, 2017, Mike left us. I set *Culture* aside and didn't reengage
it until the editor said, "The foreword is due." Reading this book is like
sitting down with Mike for coffee and continuing the conversation until
you find yourself closing the neighborhood bar at 2 a.m. I couldn't face the
realness of Mike in the words of the book. I couldn't face not being able
to ask him questions when I didn't quite understand what he had translated
from his brilliant mind to linear text.

Before his death, Mike wrote the following in a rough draft of a preface:

> So here it is, the last picture show, a little rough around the edges, a little
> out of date, but I'm running out of time. I've convinced myself that there
> at least a few good ideas worth a look, and feel that I've got a idea of cul-
> ture now that makes some kind of sense as a way to think about how the
> 21st century world works—and doesn't—as well as one way to deal with
> at least a few problems that the new global society has produced.

As usual, Mike sums it up better than I could. Thank you, Mike, for writing this book at the end of your time horizon. I will miss our conversations, but I believe your book will serve its own role in contributing to
whirled peas.

Heather Schacht Reisinger, University of Iowa

Culture

RECENTLY THE TIME HORIZON became visible—a story for another day—so I decided that I'd better work on something I really care about and work on it fast. My past projects have been called any number of things, some of them unprintable, but at their heart they always have something to do with language and culture. It goes back to my time as a high school exchange student in a small town in Austria. I had never studied German. I gave up on getting by in the local school— the classes at my age level were more sophisticated than my US high school. I couldn't have done them in English. But I did live with a family and make friends, and within those small social circles I learned enough to get by. It turns out that a particular family or a small group of friends tends to talk about the same things over and over again, so I got pretty good at it.

I only became a language and culture junkie when I registered for German class as a university freshman after I returned home. The department requested an evaluation. They didn't know what to do with me. I was more comfortable using the language than some advanced graduate students, but I was only fluent in the role of obnoxious teenager. The Prussian professor disliked me. I had never heard of Goethe, and I spoke in upper Austrian dialect. Language and culture were pretty interesting things, I decided, since the professor and I were supposedly speaking the "same language." I was doomed from that point forward to become a linguistic anthropologist who considered language and culture a problem that you had to deal with in different ways in different contexts.

Since then, I've done language–culture type work as a researcher, as an applied problem solver, and as a practitioner. Several examples from this long history will appear in the book as time goes on. But, in this book, I'm after a fundamental question. Language and culture are considered the foundation stone for the emergence of modern humans like you and me. Something to celebrate, no? But then why nowadays does it seem like those amazing abilities are often linked with conflict? Did we just stop evolving? Is there something in the early story that might explain what went wrong and how to fix it? Is it that we created a world where the old evolutionary gift of culture has turned maladaptive (if not terminally dysfunctional)?

"Culture" will get most of the airtime in this chapter. "Language" will come to center stage in the next chapter. Most scholars in the field recognize that language and culture appeared at more or less the same time in the story of human evolution. But researchers usually focus on one or the other, not on both. The culture mavens focus on things like beliefs, values, and practices of the new *Homo sapiens*. The language mavens stick more to the details of sound and grammar. I tried to fix this problem in a book in the 1990s with an awkward concept called "languaculture" (Agar, 1994). We'll return to that concept in a later chapter as well, once we get more language on the table.

In this section and the next I'll by and large follow the contours of this false dichotomy between language and culture, focusing on culture in this chapter and language in the next. Then we'll put the two together and get on with that fundamental question of why the concept of "culture" has become dysfunctional in the world today.

Embrace Vague and Ambiguous All Ye Who Enter Here

I can summarize the starting point for this section as follows: "Culture" is a frequently used mess of a concept with more meanings than there are cars on the LA freeways. It usually travels in partnership with a "problem" in today's discourse, unless you're an anthropologist, in which case it's a word you try to avoid because it's not clear what it means anymore. Culture is "an ordinary word," as Groucho used to say on his old TV show *You Bet Your Life*, "something you use every day." He always picked a "secret word" for each show, and if contestants said it, a duck fell from the ceiling and they won a hundred dollars. The way "culture" is used nowadays, it would be raining ducks if Groucho were in charge.

Culture is now promiscuously used to pretend that a problem has been described or explained when in fact it has only been squashed with a label like an insect with a flyswatter. At the same time, anthropologists—the culture professionals—routinely throw up their hands (if not their lunch) trying to make sense of what the concept might mean in our globally connected post-structural, post-colonial, post-everything world.

In this day and age, saying "culture" is like going into Las Chivas, my neighborhood coffee shop, and saying that you'd like a "cup of coffee." Coffee has so many meanings now, on the one hand, and, on the other, most of the old meanings just plain don't work anymore. Odds are good that the waitperson—I mean, the barista—will *not* respond with "Cream or sugar?" He'll say, "What kind of coffee?" and if he is kind, he'll help you along until you get to what you want: a half-decaf, half-skim double tall cappuccino on the dry side with a shot of amaretto.

The fact that "culture" has so many meanings can be verified with a week's worth of reading of popular media. You might read, just to offer a few examples, about the *culture* of gangs, the *culture* of IBM, the *culture* of Iraq, and the *culture* of Northern New Mexico. None of those uses of culture will tell you much (if anything at all) about gangs, IBM, Iraq, or Northern New Mexico. In fact, they will conceal most of what a reader might want to know if they were really interested.

In that list of examples, culture labels a loosely defined set, a collection of people who have just one attribute in common, that attribute being whatever comes after the word *of* in the phrase *culture of X*. After the labeling, we believe we know more about the labeled group than we did before. By naming it as a culture, we think we have described or explained something, a mistake rooted in the old traditional use of the concept. We think we understand a lot about the labeled group, but actually most of our prior stereotypes will survive unblemished under a new name.

From an insider's point of view, the concept can also serve political-rhetorical purposes. In management jargon, culture often means what whoever is in charge thinks our business *should* become. As another example, consider the culture of Northern New Mexico, the place I call home. It is complicated social territory, a place where a large number of histories intersect within a comparatively small population—different waves of Native Americans, Hispanics, and Anglos over the centuries, each of those labels in turn lumping together many significantly different groups, each of those groups in turn having histories of blending and intermarriage as well as separation. One often hears culture used to represent the political and economic interests of a real or imagined constituency. Culture can become a legal concept, a rallying point, a bargaining tool, or a commodity, or all four plus something else.

The traditional academic use of the culture concept isn't in much better shape. In the old days, anthropologists used it as a comprehensive and coherent label for a small-scale society and everyone in it. The Navajo, to take another New Mexico example, were called a culture. Wait a minute—not so fast.

Say a hypothetical anthropologist lived with the Navajo for a year or two, although in this case the name *Navajo* covers a lot of territory and a fairly sizable population, about 175,000 people on 27,000 square miles of reservation, and that doesn't include the more than 100,000 Navajo living elsewhere. So right away we've got the problem an older Chicano student had when I taught in Texas. He came to the office to ask a question. "You know this book you assigned, *The Mexican-Americans of South Texas?*" he asked. "Yes," I said. "Well, the title should say *some.*"

That little problem is just the tip of the iceberg. Anthropology used culture as a label that covered all of what a person was. The concept explained and generalized people as members of a particular culture, and only of that culture. Everything the anthropologist saw and heard and learned was part of Navajo culture, to stay with that hypothetical example.

A few years ago I went to the reservation for the first time, as a hiker/tourist, not as an anthropologist. I noticed in the supermarket that, by appearance alone, there were dozens of different kinds of Navajo, with everything from blue spiked hair to red velvet skirts. Then I overheard a conversation where one Navajo talked about others in terms of whether they were "traditional." The evaluation ran from yes or no to several points in between. Then a young woman told me that the real badge of identity was a personal connection through kin to the Long Walk, when the United States relocated the tribe in the nineteenth century to what was in fact a concentration camp. She didn't mention language or clan, which is what I'd expected to hear. She reminded me more of exile and return and Holocaust conversations I'd had with Israelis than of anything I'd read about the Navajo.

This superficial vignette is enough for the moral of the story. Anyone now, Navajo or anyone else, is a mix of cultures of many different sorts, and the mix can vary from one situation to another, and the person can vary in their attitude toward different parts of the mix, and any particular culture in the mix is probably debated and changing from the point of view of its members. An African American call-in radio show in Baltimore, for example, fascinated me, an old white guy working in that city. I listened to callers debate, day after day, what it meant to be black. It meant something to everyone, but exactly what it meant varied all over the place.

The old image of culture fired the anthropological imagination for decades. Not so long ago, professors of anthropology were still hunting for the last primitive culture. Some readers may have read about the madness around the discovery of the so-called Gentle Tasaday in the Philippines in the early 1970s. Anthropologists, and many others, wanted to believe that a genuine *primitive* culture still existed in the modern world. The discovery was followed by accusations of fraud, that a local rich guy paid some indigenous people to imitate an undiscovered isolated tribe. A more recent book tells the convoluted and controversial story (Hemley, 2003).

In the 1990s I was lucky enough to have a chance to chat with a justice of the supreme court in Palau. The island nation had achieved independence from the United States in 1994. I was visiting the country as a tourist/diver, but a Palauan colleague in public health had invited me to a few social events. When the justice learned I was an anthropologist, he told me a story about the late William Gladwin, an anthropologist who had done fieldwork for years in Micronesia, a man whose personal integrity and scholarly work was (and still is) among the most admired in the field. He had helped out as an unpaid consultant, at Palau's invitation, to make the transition from United Nations protectorate under US administration to a "Compact of Free Association." The justice's affection for Gladwin was obvious. But, he said, the anthropologist was too biased toward traditional culture when it came to drafting the new constitution. The island, said the justice, had to acknowledge it, but they couldn't build a late twentieth-century nation on the basis of ancestral custom.

In anthropology it is not news that the old culture concept doesn't work anymore. The old concept carries connotations of a closed system, frozen in time, with a comprehensive and consistent image of what a person is and how he/she should act. No more. Nowadays the term of art is "globalization," as it is in many other popular and professional conversations and writings around the world. And globalization means we have to rethink the old idea of culture when we talk about a particular person or a particular group. A person nowadays isn't just wrapped in a single culture. A person nowadays is wrapped in . . . what?

The Palauan justice's argument is also the argument of this book. Culture has become part of the problem, not part of the solution. Now cultures are loose cannons, or was that canons, of many calibers in the social fields of our global world. This mixing and matching and resulting conflict among what we think of as cultures has acquired some different names. One, made popular in the work of Néstor García Canclini, is the word *hybrid* (2005). Hybrid has some meanings that others object to. In fact, some people prefer words like *creole* (Hannerz, 1987), on the analogy with creole languages that formed from blends of a local and a colonial language.

For my purposes here, I'll stick with the term *hybrid*, with one modification on the dictionary definition: "A thing made by combining two different elements; a mixture." The modification is that there can be many more than just two elements in the mix. Take me, for instance: I'm of a generational culture—a 1960s college student, early baby boomer, retirement age. I'm of Chicago Irish ancestry on my father's side, unknown on my mother's, but the Irish part was never emphasized growing up, and one great-grandfather started out Protestant in Ireland. A recent DNA test says I'm 27 percent Ashkenazi, something of a surprise to a former altar boy. I'm a recovering Catholic who went to Catholic grammar school. I've lived and worked in Austria so much over the years that I'm part Austrian in a weird way. I've worked in the streets with heroin addicts. I've been a scuba diver for decades. I'm an old white guy. Santa Fe, where I live now, is the first place I've ever lived where "wacky old white guy" is a recognized ethnic group.

As an old friend of mine used to joke, but enough about *me*, how do *you* like my new hairdo? This list of labels now used as cultural tags has only just begun. There are many, many more. All of those "culture" categories are labels someone might use to explain things I do or say. More than one will be relevant to any moment of explanation. To make things worse, the way any number of them mixes with the other will vary from time to time. Worse still, my relationship to any of those labels changes over time and will continue to do so. Worst of all, I regularly meet people, also members of one or more of the categories I belong in, with whom I have little in common, sometimes to the point where membership in the same category makes no sense.

I'm a multiple *cultural hybrid*. So is any reader of this book. I'll bet a large amount of money that the members of the Gentle Tasaday (the "primitive" tribe mentioned earlier) are as well—certainly by now in the early twenty-first century. They have become what one anthropologist called "professional primitives" (Fox, 1969), among many other things.

So we are stuck with problems—often called "cultural" but also problems of "diversity" or "social exclusion" or any number of other ways of putting it—that are the results of our human world changing from isolated groups of hunter-gatherers to a global society. And the same changes that knit the world into a global society—war, trade, neoliberalism, migration, technology—have made the culture concept difficult to use to solve the problems these historical forces have produced. The culture concept doesn't apply in a straightforward and coherent way to hybrids that recent global history has bred in increasing number.

The problem is that we can't use a concept that doesn't work with hybrids to fix a "culture" problem. To cite a famous Einstein quote, "We can't solve problems by using the same kind of thinking we used when we created them." This book returns to hybrids in a big way later, especially in the last two chapters. First, though, we need to do some more work on the culture concept to learn more about what we're dealing with.

Diversity, You Say?

I'm an anthropologist, so when it comes to human variation in beliefs or practices I automatically think "culture." But most people are not anthropologists, fortunately for the world, and when they think of human variation they use words in addition to "culture" to mean more or less the same thing.

For example, many in the real world talk more about human variation in terms of "diversity" instead of culture, another cliché of our day. Figure 1.1 is a picture of the diversity dream from a business perspective: a group of smiling young people affirming their unity, like an NFL team

Figure 1.1.
Source: iStock Essentials/Vasyl Dolmatov

right before the kickoff, only with more simpatico expressions on their faces. There are three men and three women. One man and one woman are white, while the other two men and women are people of color, although a different color from each other, all portrayed with politically correct algorithmic precision. Research, claim the organizational theory types, shows that diverse teams will be more creative and make better decisions when compared with—I don't know what to call them—the non-diverse, the uni-verse?

This might be right under certain conditions and terribly wrong under others. I remember working in Baltimore, a majority African American city. I worked with a group where most colleagues were black. The United States—where recent events around police shootings have made the headlines—is a racially charged nation, a long-standing fact obvious to most everyone. It took a couple of months for everybody in the project to get past suspicion and caution and eventually land in trust. The key seemed to be getting to the point where if someone said something insulting or just plain stupid, everyone assumed it wasn't malicious and treated it with humor. The change was about the development of reputation and trust, a theme we will return to. Once we got to that point, we did get very creative. Different perspectives provided many more ingredients for a solution to whatever problem we were dealing with than any single perspective alone could have.

Diversity isn't the only alternative name for culture-like issues. Some Europeans talk more in terms of inclusion and exclusion. (See http://www .inclusionexclusion.nl/site/ for an example.) Elsewhere the phrase *identity politics* has become cultivated territory, meaning the organization of a political movement to struggle against injustice on the part of some category of person. The online *Stanford Encyclopedia of Philosophy* will enlighten you on its history and current shapes (see Heyes 2018).

I hope to convince you that a rose by any other name would smell as sweet, to steal a line from Shakespeare. This book is about culture, among other things, but it is more general than that. It is about anything in our contemporary terminological jungle that names conflict arising from human variation.

All of these perspectives—and many others—see culture, or diversity, or inclusion, as an *issue*, a problem, a new characteristic of modern life that needs to be recognized, understood, and dealt with. In the spirit of "inclusion," I will continue to use the term *diversity*, just in this section, to show you what I mean. Whenever you see diversity, you should be able to substitute cultural differences, as far as popular discourse goes.

But why is diversity a problem? Haven't different kinds of people gotten along in the past? Or at least tolerated each other? Of course they have. But in the past there were bounded diversity spaces. Port towns or centers of trade or capitals of empire are classic examples, spaces where political and religious and commercial interests required the presence of very different kinds of people. Such bounded spaces existed in microscopic versions as well. The famous bar scene from *Star Wars* is an interplanetary version. And I remember when I read Herman Melville's novel *Moby-Dick*—what a diverse crew that ship had.

One reason diversity feels different now is because *diversity spaces are no longer bounded*. Everywhere on Earth is a diversity space. The term no longer sorts things out, because diversity is everywhere.

Another reason diversity feels different is because of *rhythm*. In the past, a new population would appear, and time would pass as they fit into and altered the local historical flow. Where I live now in New Mexico, the Athabascan Indians—ancestors of the Navajo and the Apache—rolled into the land of the Pueblo Indians by 1500 (some say earlier than that). The Puebloans themselves, who arrived thousands of years ago, speak several languages, so it isn't hard to imagine diversity issues at ceremonial sites like Chaco and Mesa Verde. The first Spanish settlement was founded in 1598. The Americans annexed the Southwest in 1848. Now Santa Fe officially celebrates its tricultural identity in tourist brochures, though the predictable tensions brew under the myth and occasionally blow through the surface like historical magma. But at least all those diverse groups had some time to get used to each other, for better or for worse.

It's not like that anymore. Diversity shifts and moves like an amoeba on steroids. Encounters with *new* diversity in one's lifetime will likely happen many times, often indirectly (if not directly). The rhythm of diversity has accelerated from whole notes with a couple of full rests to a twelve-bar flurry of sixteenth notes that make for what jazz genius John Coltrane called sheets of sound.

Diversity has gone from bounded to everywhere and from infrequent to continuous. Maybe it's not quite that dramatic, but it often feels that way. The reason so many people and organizations all over the world are suddenly worried about diversity is that it's everywhere, all the time.

Diversity is a problem, something a lot of different people and organizations think they need to do something about. Listen to the complaints, and it's obvious that diversity is used to explain why something isn't working right. What isn't working right? How do you tell? Things don't get done as easily as they used to. It's not that anyone necessarily or even usually has a personal goal to disrupt those things—I'll use *tasks* as the general cover term for things that people are doing at any particular moment. True, there are always some people around who enjoy destroying a task, with or without diversity. That's the universal and eternal problem of what to do with the terminally obnoxious and the town drunk.

No, people, usually with good intentions at first, have different notions of what a particular task actually is and different expectations of how one should go about doing it. More and more often, diverse people suddenly, perhaps surprisingly, find themselves doing the same task together, perhaps face-to-face, perhaps at a distance spanning half the globe. On a local level they work together. They live together. They go to the same school. When they get sick they go to the same hospital, and when they get in trouble they deal with the same police department and court system. They vote in the same elections, in places that have them, and they fill out the same tax forms. On a global level they often buy the same products—wherever they live—work for the same international companies, eat at the same restaurants, suffer the same wars, have the same media, articulate the same ideology, travel to the same places for vacation, and (if they are highfliers) buy and sell in the same global markets.

But all those people sharing a task do not see things the same way. They have different *perspectives*, on what they believe, on what they value, on how they feel, on the general way they think things should be done, and on the specific details of what any particular task involves. The differences might be trivial and easily change. "Oh, sure, sorry, didn't know that's how things worked here." Or the differences might be deep-seated, learned as a child and used habitually as an adolescent until they became the natural order of things. "What? That's ridiculous. No one in their right mind would do things that way."

The original good intentions can turn into annoyance and ferment into anger. For a person who grew up in a specific place, it can turn into hatred of outsiders. For a new arrival, it can turn into feelings of persecution and intolerance. For people at a distance, it can turn into censorship of media and outsider contact. For any person trying to do a task with others, it can turn into frustration that makes them want to do the task only with people who think and act just like them. Taken to extremes, it turns into war. Tasks that started with purpose and value go straight to hell in a handcart.

Sometimes the intentions and expectations are poisoned from the start. An ancient historical event turned into a myth that fuels generations of hatred, an image of *those people* crystallized and hardened from real past experiences of oppression into a need for scapegoats to explain why something in life has gone wrong. This is the culture-diversity problem with teeth in it, harder to change because it's a core part of who the malcontents think they are.

Historical events or past experiences may have left a residue of lives gone terribly wrong. The theft of an ancestor's land, commerce that destroyed the usual way of making a living, invaders forcing aside at gunpoint beliefs and values that define who you are—or, rather, were. The diversity problem might have deep roots indeed.

How do we even begin to untangle all these "cultural" or "diversity" issues? Are they "cultural" at all? What could it possibly mean to say that? That's why I wrote this book: to try for a different angle on this so-called diversity problem, to try and understand better where culture came from by going back in the origins of modern humanity about fifty thousand years ago, one traditional estimate of culture's debut now turned controversial, an issue we'll revisit later in the book.

The emphasis in this book will be on how people with different perspectives—call them diverse or culturally different—might better handle that diversity. If enough people handle it better—either because of something in this book or because they figure out something better—things will improve long before any policies or programs accomplish anything. My motto for change is a quote from a three-by-five card that I saw tacked to the wall of a waterfront Texas bar. The card said, "I must go, for there go my people, and I am their leader." Oddly enough, the card paraphrases a famous quote from Gandhi.

You see what I mean about culture? What's Gandhi doing on the wall of an oysterman's bar?

It's Hard to Fix Culture with Culture

In spite of all the problems using the culture concept, this article of faith endures: Culture is causing problems, and therefore culture is where we can fix them. This premise has grown like kudzu over the course of my student and professional life. "Intercultural communication" became a publishing and consulting gold mine, as did fields related to other terms used in this book like "diversity training."

Several years ago, at the point when the US adventures in Afghanistan and Iraq were starting to be widely recognized as the catastrophes they so obviously are, I was invited to be a plenary speaker at an all-military workshop. One of the organizers had read my book *Language Shock*.

More interesting than the presentations were the conversations with officers of my age from different branches of the military. They, like me, had been shaped by the Vietnam War. In quiet sidebar conversations they said they couldn't tell the secretary of defense and the commander-in-chief that they were naïve fucking idiots. They needed people like me and the other invited intercultural experts to say it for them. One guy actually used those words; the others put it more politely.

The problem, they said, was culture. Their professional lives as warriors had been distorted by naïveté about Vietnamese "culture." The current Afghan/Iraq story, they felt, was a replay of the same problem. The answer? Teach military and civilians about the culture of a place before doing anything about it. As one snarky Brit put it, "War is God's way of teaching Americans geography."

That experience led to a couple of projects that showed how "culture" was difficult to use to solve problems that it itself had created. I was part of a team assembled to design a "serious" video game. Its purpose? To teach different communication styles to American NGOs and military on their way to Afghanistan about the "cultural differences" that an American would likely encounter.

Anyone who knows Afghanistan also knows how insane it is to try and describe the country in terms of a single "culture." Not to mention generalizing the American culture of the students in a way that made any sense. And anyone who knows the country will also know the saying that Afghanistan is "the graveyard of empires." An Anglo-European face of an economic development expert is just another in a long line of English, Russian, and now American faces with ambitions to run the country, no matter how he or she talks.

The team I worked with, all oriented toward the details of language, did an exemplary job of creating a game even given the destructive micromanagement and flaky fiscal behavior of the federal security agencies we dealt with. But, in the end, the game wasn't going to solve the intercultural problem. While I was working on the project, there was a scandal in Afghanistan when some American soldiers burned copies of the Koran. Had they known how to open a conversation and speak indirectly—the lessons of the game we developed—I doubt it would've made much difference. As a cynical friend teased me, "Whoops, you forgot to tell them not to burn the holy book of Islam."

Is there any way to use the culture concept to solve rather than cause problems? Especially in this day and age? People doing the same task together are probably hybrids under the influence of multiple cultures that differ in fundamental ways—even within themselves—in how that task in particular is supposed to work. But, maybe, if we invest some preliminary labor on the definitions that most people don't worry about when they use the "C" word, we can make use of the "culture" concept.

Going back to the old days, culture never meant just one thing in anthropology but two—neither of them well defined, but at least there were only two. One meaning was what we've been talking about so far—for now, let's just say the beliefs and practices of a specific group. In the old days, a "specific group" was a small, poor, isolated community in the "third world." But a second meaning was that culture labeled those abilities that differentiate humans from other animals. All humans have culture; no animals do—that was the simple assumption in the old days that we're going to undermine in this book.

In graduate school, the study of specific groups was emphasized. The more general concept—culture as what it meant to be human—was neglected. In fact, it was amazingly simple to mistake a piece of one's own particular culture for what must be true of all of humanity, a widely distributed personal problem called "ethnocentrism." It is just this second version of culture—what humans have in common—that offers common ground for connection no matter what the culture-specific differences might be.

Culture, Big *C* and Little *c*

Something remarkable happened about fifty thousand years ago, something that really does look like it set humans off from the rest of the animal kingdom. Compared with the four and a half billion years the Earth has been around, the modern human story hasn't gone on all that long. By one set of estimates, hominins—awkward jargon for the human line—split off from the chimps about five million years ago. Major changes happened along the way, from more ape-like to more human-like, from one tool technology to another. But, by and large, changes were slow, and, once they occurred, they looked similar wherever they were found by archaeologists many millennia later.

But starting about fifty thousand years ago, and increasing from then on, this slow pace of change sped up dramatically. With this turning point, the experts start talking about *Homo sapiens sapiens* instead of just *Homo sapiens*. They didn't just look like us, as the earlier *Homo sapiens* had—they acted like us as well. (Some recent work argues that the sharp dividing line between *Homo sapiens'* emergence about two hundred thousand years ago and the appearance of *Homo sapiens sapiens'* culture about fifty thousand years ago no longer holds. I'm going to use *Homo sapiens* for both. Context will make clear what time period is being discussed.)

> Before 50,000 years ago, human anatomy and human behavior appear to have evolved relatively slowly, more or less in concert. After 50,000 years ago, anatomical evolution all but ceased, while behavioral evolution accelerated dramatically. Now, for the first time, humans possessed the full-blown capacity for culture, based on an almost infinite ability to innovate. They had evolved a unique capacity to adapt to environment not through their anatomy or physiology but through culture. Cultural evolution began to follow its own trajectory, and it took the fast track. Even as our bodies have changed little in the past 50,000 years, culture has evolved at an astonishing and ever-accelerating rate. (Klein & Edgar, 2002, p. 21)

Notice that Klein and Edgar say fifty thousand years ago. Others say forty thousand, as you'll see in quotes to come. In fact, the current argument pushes the date back even further. *Homo sapiens* emerged about two hundred thousand years ago, and one of the great mysteries of evolution has been why it took one hundred fifty thousand years to get culture going. Nowadays the hypothesis is that the objects usually taken as evidence of culture's emergence appeared much earlier in the archaeological record. We'll see later that the takeoff curve allows for this. For now, I'll stick with the less controversial date range, forty to fifty thousand years ago, give or take a couple of months.

Klein and Edgar call this remarkable transition the "Culture Big Bang," a term I will frequently borrow in this book. Jared Diamond, in his book *The Third Chimpanzee*, calls it the "Great Leap Forward" (2006). Harris and Johnson, in their introduction to cultural anthropology, describe it as a "cultural takeoff": "After cultural 'takeoff,' the rate of *cultural evolution* increased dramatically without any concurrent increase in the rate of human biological evolution. The occurrence of cultural 'takeoff' justifies the contention of most anthropologists that to understand the last 40,000 years of the evolution of culture, primary emphasis must be given to cultural rather than biological processes" (2007, p. 40; emphasis in original).

Merlin Donald, in his book on cognitive evolution, writes, "Humans are better and faster at everything: social coordination, tool manufacture, systematic war, finding and building shelter, gathering and hunting food" (1993, p. 210). Living spaces became more organized. Humans buried their dead with more ritual. Production of clothing out of hides improved. Hunting became more sophisticated. Tool making developed, and ornamental figures and jewelry appeared. The Culture Big Bang allowed humans to "extract far more energy from nature and to invest it in society. It also allowed human populations to colonize new and challenging environments. Possibly the most critical aspect of the neural change was that it allowed the kind of rapidly spoken phonemic language that is inseparable from culture as we know it today. This ability not only facilitates communication, but at least equally important, it allows people to conceive and model complex natural and social circumstances entirely within their minds" (Klein & Edgar, 2002, p. 24). Notice the emphasis on language in this quote. Historically, anthropology considered culture and language as the domain of two distinct subfields. As a result, discussions of cultural evolution and linguistic evolution are often kept separate from each other. I'm going to follow this artificial distinction in this chapter and the next, though the next chapter on language will begin to merge the two into a single phenomenon.

We used to say that this increased pace of innovation and change marked the birth of both culture and language. We still do, but that claim is more complicated now. We know that animals can cogitate and communicate much more than we ever thought they could and that hominins before *Homo sapiens* could, too. But even though our claim now shows more respect to our human ancestors and animal contemporaries, the data still show that *Homo sapiens* made some kind of evolutionary leap. Whatever they started with that they shared with animals and earlier humans, they took it well beyond anything that had happened before.

What was this something that made the difference? A number of researchers have suggested answers to this question over the years. I don't mean to review and evaluate them all in this book. The hypothesis here, born of reading a sample of evolutionary experts and bringing in my own background in linguistics, will run like this: Humans developed a more elaborate *generative ability*, an ability to look at a task, analyze it into parts, recombine those parts in a different way and create new ones, and change the task, for better or for worse. We'll see that this ability had its roots in what earlier hominins could do, and we'll see as the book goes on that language worked particularly well to help it along.

But then something also had to evolve to keep this new ability in check. If the new humans started generating away, every moment of every day, early *Homo sapiens* would have looked like a faculty meeting and accomplished about as much. Something had to coevolve with the new generative ability to *constrain* it and keep it under control, but without at the same time destroying it. Those constraints, as I will argue later in this chapter, gave rise to culture in the way that we usually talk about it now—culture as a system to rein us in and glue us together into small groups.

Generativity was part of the new universal human ability that we call culture. Constraints held the innovations that were generated together into local clusters. We call those local clusters "culture," too. The trend in my lifetime, in anthropology, has been a shift in research from the local culture to culture as something characteristic of humans in general. Local culture is what causes the problems; human culture is where we might find some solutions. Such is the argument I hope to develop here.

Growing "culture" Out of "Culture"

In the next few sections, I'm going to write about *generative* and *constraint mechanisms* and how they balance each other out. Or, rather, how they used to but don't so well anymore because hybrids mix things up. I know that a lot of people don't care for the term *mechanism*. It does call up images of machinery, of Charlie Chaplin spinning around in the gears of a machine in the movie *Modern Times*. Many people prefer the term *process*. The truth is that *process* isn't that clean a term, either. Since I recently learned some Argentinean history, I'm sensitive to it. The generals called it *el proceso militar* when they disappeared several thousand Argentines in the 1970s. If that isn't bad enough for you, the original German title of Kafka's novel *The Trial* is *Der Prozess*. Then there's *processed* food. How about a Velveeta and Spam sandwich while you wait for the midnight knock on the door and the kangaroo court that follows? As far as connotations go (for me, anyway), *mechanism* beats *process* by a country mile, and so that's the word I'll use.

Once the Culture Big Bang occurred, "the great increase in artifactual diversity through time and space provides the oldest concrete indication for ethnographic 'cultures' or identity-conscious ethnic groups" (Klein & Edgar, 2002, p. 233). As they often do, Klein and Edgar use the term *innovate* as a key description of what happened. They write that, in Africa as well as in Europe and Asia, "innovations included solidly built houses, tailored clothing, more efficient fireplaces, and new hunting technology" (p. 235).

Homo sapiens did things differently when compared to the Neanderthals in Europe and the early modern humans in Africa. They became more innovative, more creative, more capable of experimenting with new possibilities. If I were naming *Homo sapiens*, I'd call them the *tinkering* humans: *Homo tinkerus*. The Oxford American dictionary defines *tinker* as an "attempt to repair or improve something in a casual or desultory way, often to no useful effect." "Often," but not "always." Tinkering strikes me as exactly the right word for what *Homo sapiens* started to do.

This new human ability to tinker, to innovate, to generate, is called *culture*. Notice how different this is from the usual contemporary use of the term. *Culture* in the phrase "Culture Big Bang" doesn't mean the unique beliefs and practices of a particular group. Instead, it labels something that evolved as part and parcel of the human condition, a new ability that earlier humans and animals did not have, certainly not to the same extent. This ability—call it *Culture with a capital C*—is another name for the ability to *generate*. It means to step back, analyze a task, reconfigure it, and do it a different way.

As we'll see again and again in this book, there is a slippery slope here along the human-animal border. The example in the image below dates back to the early twentieth century. Wolfgang Köhler, a founder of Gestalt psychology, showed that chimps had a generative streak in them as well. In figure 1.2, Sultan has analyzed the situation and figured out that if he puts

Figure 1.2.
Source: Psychestudy

some sticks together, he can reach the food hanging outside of his reach. This generative ability shown by animals is, however, less sophisticated than that of humans.

Culture with a capital *C* allowed for the creation of cultures with a small *c*, what Klein and Edgar described earlier as "identity-conscious ethnic groups in the modern sense" and "ethnographic 'cultures.'" The new generative ability set each hunting-gathering band off on its own trajectory, its own history of tinkering with a task to change how it was done. Within a single human lifetime, brief as it was in those days, several changes might occur in how various tasks were done. Language of course was also part of the universal human story, a part left until the next chapter, but a part that also grew into *different* forms within each hunting-gathering group.

Culture with a capital C, the new generative ability of all *Homo sapiens*, made it possible for what we now think of as cultural differences to appear. To distinguish those group-specific differences from Culture with a capital *C*, I'll call them *cultures with a small c*. Culture with a small *c* means that different hunting-gathering bands put the new ability to different uses. Changes over time took "small-*c* cultures" in different directions depending on how they started and what they needed to do next in their local worlds. The development of variety among cultures with a small *c* is what archaeologists discovered in the variation in the archeological record starting roughly fifty thousand years ago.

Cultural diversity was born out of a universal human ability to make and change a culture. This book will argue that that universal ability is where the contemporary solution to cultural diversity lies. When problems arise as a function of conflict among cultures with a small *c* in the same task, the answer isn't to tinker with the details of the small-*c* cultures in question. The answer—or so this book will argue—will be to scale up into the superordinate category that includes all local small-*c* versions, what we're calling culture with a capital *C*, the basis for the shared humanity of those who are having the problem in the first place. That's where similarities are guaranteed to be found.

What changed, about fifty thousand years ago, were the number and type of innovations across many different tasks that varied from group to group. The archaeological record shows more effective hunting techniques and better ability to survive the harsh environments of the Late Stone Age/ Upper Paleolithic. It shows more cooperation in raising children. It shows population growth and longer life expectancy, care of the sick and funerary rituals for the dead. And of course the cave art and jewelry and flutes.

The innovations increased evolutionary success for some bands, which in turn selected for an increase in ability to innovate, which then improved evolutionary success. That's the kind of *positive*—or *amplifying*—feedback loop that makes things increase at an accelerated rate. It put the "bang" in "Culture Big Bang."

But the term *evolution* now has to expand beyond the biological. It's no longer only a matter of genetic inheritance with variation and natural selection. Anthropologists coined the term *dual inheritance theory* (DIT) to recognize this fact (Boyd & Richerson, 1985). After the Big Bang, culture with a small *c* could be changed, by human will alone, at a speed limit that left the slow pace of natural selection in the dust, all thanks to culture with a capital *C*. (More on DIT later.)

Generativity

In his book on cognitive evolution, Donald draws on Michael Corballis's version of generativity. Generativity is both an analytic and a combinatorial skill. The argument is summarized in Corballis's book *From Hand to Mouth* (2003).

Generativity, so goes the hypothesis, was the key mechanism that enabled innovation to increase dramatically. It produced all that variation in the archaeological data that supports the argument for the Culture Big Bang. The first part of Corballis's definition of generativity has to do with *analysis*. What does analysis mean? It means realizing that something is not just what it appears to be in isolation. It means seeing a *whole* in terms of *parts*, in one of two different ways.

The obvious way is that the whole is seen as made up of other things. It consists of a number of interlinked parts. Perception shifts one level of scale *down* to the next lower level. Analysis changes the question from "What is this mechanism?" to "What is this mechanism made of?" and "How does it work?"

A second way to look at analysis: The *whole* is seen as *part of* some larger mechanism. It is seen in terms of what it contributes to in the bigger scheme of things. Analysis shifts the question from "What is this mechanism?" to "How does this mechanism work as a part in some larger mechanism?" and "What role does it play?" It shifts perception one level of scale *up* to the next higher level.

Let me entertain you with a bourgeois example. It is more about tools than it is about social routines, but it makes the point. I only recently became a homeowner—home-*moaner*, my brother calls it. I've been an urban apartment renter most of my life. Many things that I saw as a whole when I lived in a rented apartment I have now learned to see as a bunch of parts. To use Heidegger's famous line, you don't know what a hammer is until it breaks and there is no landlord to call. He didn't say that last part, but he must have been a homeowner.

There's a garage door opener that isn't just a garage door opener. It has a little electric eye light in the lower corner with a bulb that burns out, I learned while working on a draft of this chapter, at which point the opener quits and you have to figure out which parts to move which way so you can open and close the door by hand. And the outdoor faucet—it has a valve to prevent back pressure. It jams if dirt gets in there, an event that caused ethical dilemmas when the plumber pointed out he could just shoot some epoxy in and the hell with it. And caulk? Don't get me started. I own more tubes of caulk now than I do socks.

Why are all you homeowners laughing? These are classic cases of shifting from a holistic view to an analytic view. Not to mention shifting from a rented city apartment to your own home in the burbs. It's how you learn to fix something that you never had to fix before, because you thought of the thing as a whole rather than as a system of parts.

Here's a bourgeois example in the other direction, seeing the whole as part of something larger. As a renter, I didn't pay property taxes—not directly. Now that I'm a homeowner, I do. Now when a list of issues appears on the ballot that requires a new property tax assessment, I pay attention. Am I willing to pay more for a new school when I don't have any school-age kids? Self-interest versus community support becomes personal rather than abstract.

This ability to *analyze*—the first part of generativity—took off and generalized to all domains of life as part and parcel of the Culture Big Bang. And it wouldn't have just applied to objects. It would have generated music, art, more complicated social relations, and religious ritual as well. Seeing wholes in terms of parts and vice versa can—emphasis on *possibility*—lead to changing the whole to make life better in any number of ways, better in many senses of the word, or of course also possibly worse, as in "If it ain't broke, don't fix it."

And some applications of generativity would have changed things just for the hell of it. They might not have served critical goals of food and sex, but they might not have gotten in the way, either. Even biologists say that most characteristics of a species are *not* the result of natural selection. They're the result of what they call *genetic drift* (i.e., changes that seem to serve no evolutionary advantage), something especially common in small populations. It's easy to imagine that those early bands of hunter-gatherers produced a substantial amount of *cultural drift* as well. The concept has been around in anthropology for a while (Eggan, 1963).

Whatever the application, though, analysis means that the mechanism in question is made up of parts rather than an irreducible whole. It also means the mechanism can be seen as a part of something larger. It can go either way. Whichever way it goes, analysis opens up the possibility of new *combinations*—the second part of generativity according to Corballis's definition. Humans become what I called *Homo tinkerus*. Parts can be used and new ones can be created to be combined and recombined and added to and subtracted from in different ways to change the nature of the whole.

Now that you're aware of the separate pieces, *how can you put them together in a different way?* According to one definition, combinatorics is "the branch of mathematics studying the enumeration, combination, and permutation of sets of elements and the mathematical relations that characterize their properties" (http://mathworld.wolfram.com/Combinatorics .html). Analysis takes care of the *enumeration* part of the definition. Combinatorics then shows the many ways that the parts can be reshuffled into different combinations.

In the Culture Big Bang, new combinatorial possibilities opened up the world of tinkering, of trying something different that might improve the performance of a particular task. Let me illustrate with another bourgeois story from the life of the new homeowner. I should add that my father was a photographer. His idea of training me to fix things was to pick up the phone. Smart man. However, he used a beer can opener to open film cassettes rather than buying an expensive tool at the store.

My house has an old wooden screen door. The first summer I lived in it, the door had shrunk so much that a crack opened at the top and many winged creatures started commuting inside. Never in my life had I thought of a screen door as anything more than a screen door. It just hangs there and lets fresh air in. So I stared at it and tried to imagine parts that would fix the sag, or fill the gap, or something. For the first time in my life, I was deeply into screen door analysis.

I won't bore you with all the things I thought of. You're probably bored enough already, unless you're a homeowner who enjoys the occasional moment of *schadenfreude*. After an extensive period of screen door meditation, I wondered why there wasn't a part that was kind of a stick that mounted crossways at an angle from the hinge side of the door to pull the sagging corner up. I went to the hardware store, and it turned out there was such a thing. Not many of them, because screen doors tend to be metal now, not wood. So I bought it and took it home and adjusted it, and it worked like a charm.

This example shows the results of tinkering with new combinations based on what one comes up with by analyzing a whole. It also shows how we can imagine parts that might be there but aren't. Humans aren't limited to just the parts that they come up with from the analysis of the moment. They can combine and recombine those, of course. But they can also imagine other parts that aren't there, or discard parts that are. They don't *just* do combinations of what is in the set, like the mathematical definition says. They *change* what is in the set as well.

Gregory Bateson's concept of *deutero-learning* offers a classic way to think about this change (2000). To translate his concept into the discussion here, I'll call it *combinatorial learning*. Imagine that at a particular time a person can choose among some arrangement of parts. If he or she *changes* the arrangement, that would be one kind of learning. Straightforward generativity. Simple analysis and combination. That kind of rock makes a better tool than this kind. This kind of screw holds the screen door better than that kind. This car gets better mileage than that car.

But now suppose that a person doesn't just change the combination. They change what's *in* the set of available parts to make a new combination. Now there's a different set of parts, new ones that weren't in the set before and old ones that have disappeared. Instead of picking a better rock, let's try a stick. Instead of a screw, let's glue it on. Instead of a car, let's buy a bike.

The late Waldo the cat offers a good example of the difference. One day I came in to feed him, and he'd chewed an almost geometrically perfect head-sized hole in the side of a bag of cat food sitting on the counter. That was pretty good tinkering on his part. But when a door was installed to let him go in and out of a window, it took a long time and a lot of unsubtle training before he finally got it. He preferred to continue sitting on the back porch, yelling for someone to open the sliding door. Eventually, after a lot of work, and a lot of undignified shoving and scratching, Waldo combinatorial-learned, but it took a while, and his humans had to force him into it, over and over again.

Humans, by contrast, combinatorial-learn all the time. Once *Homo sapiens* developed generativity, they could do combinatorics in more sophisticated ways than animals and earlier forms of humanity ever had before. The combinatorial possibilities increased, not only because *Homo sapiens* saw wholes in terms of parts but also because they imagined new parts that weren't there and saw old parts as items to be discarded. The temperamental artist and the idiot savant were born.

Analysis and *combination*. Generativity mixes the two into a key mechanism that produced the Culture Big Bang. But generativity also created a problem—namely, the potential for chaos. Imagine if our ancestors had turned on the generativity and never slowed it down. If generativity just took off like that, *unconstrained*, the Culture Big Bang would not have been a Great Leap Forward, as Jared Diamond called it. It would have been the explosive end of the *Homo sapiens* experiment. We might all be Neanderthals now, or possibly a nonhuman branch of the great apes. Maybe the better for it.

Let me mention a couple of contemporary global examples to show the consequences of unconstrained innovation. Consider the so-called war on drugs. The primary constraint, supported by budget and public opinion, has always been law enforcement. It has failed, spectacularly and repeatedly. Innovations in production and distribution have continued since the "war" was declared in 1971. As my colleagues in law enforcement often said, "The bad guys are always one step ahead of us." With such a high-revenue dependency-producing product, law enforcement has proven incapable of constraining illegal-drug epidemics. Another example is the current planet-wide environmental crisis caused by explosive technological innovation since the Industrial Revolution and especially since the 1950s. The lack of constraints on environmental damage may well have pushed us beyond our ability to repair it.

Constraint Mechanisms

To explain why our ancestors did not in fact self-destruct, I need to introduce a second family of mechanisms that innovation produced, what I'll call *constraint mechanisms*. These mechanisms are *conservative* rather than innovative. They slow that innovation curve down with dampening or negative feedback loops. While generativity sparkles with new possibilities, constraints muffle them, apply the brakes, and try to keep generativity under control.

The difference between the two mechanisms correlates roughly with an *individual* level versus a *social* level. In general, an individual does generativity. An individual takes a look, analyzes, combines in a new and different way, and creates a way of doing something. The key innovator is usually a person. Not always, though. A group might sit around and collectively analyze and combine. The concept of "brainstorming" is a case in point. There's a famous scene in the movie *Apollo 13*: The boys in the space capsule are in trouble. The boss back on the ground walks into a room full of engineers. He lays down some material. "This is what they've got to work with," he says. "This is the problem they have. Figure out how they can fix it." Classic collective generativity, though I'll bet there were one or two generative leaders in the group.

But, by and large, some person usually has the bright idea first. At least that's my hypothesis. William James expressed this concept well: "Social evolution is a resultant of the interaction of two wholly distinct factors: the individual, deriving his peculiar gifts from the play of physiological and infra-social forces, but bearing all the power of initiative and origination in his own hands; and second, the social environment, with its power of adopting or rejecting both him and his gifts. Both factors are essential to change" (1880, p. 448).

Constraint mechanisms, as we'll see in the next several chapters, are more *social* than individual. Several experiments dramatize how social mechanisms shape and control individual perception and action. But here, too, things aren't quite so clear-cut. Except for psychopaths, individuals also carry social constraints around with them. Freud called it the superego; George Herbert Mead called it the generalized other. Foucault created a theory of governance out of it, and Bourdieu, illustrating the tendency of researchers to isolate themselves by creating opaque jargon, called it "doxa." In fact, the question of how a person incorporates society into their sense of self has been one of the major themes of social theory since its inception.

For present purposes, I only want to take a look at the *general* idea of constraints. *Constraint* is an ordinary word, used in many domains—for example, in mathematics to business to everyday conversation. My dictionary defines it as a limitation or restriction. Mathematicians see it as an inequality—the number of glasses of wine I drink with dinner should be two or less if I'm driving (i.e., "$N < 3$"). Washington colleagues use the term to define politics as the art of the possible. Sherlock Holmes translated it into the principle that if you eliminate all possibilities but one, then that one has to be true.

The general argument is this: The constraint mechanisms that evolved with the Culture Big Bang made sense as a way to stabilize generativity in hunting-gathering bands in Late Stone Age/Upper Paleolithic environments. But the same mechanisms that produced those cultures with a small *c* are now maladaptive in contemporary global society. We *Homo sapiens* still need constraints to balance generativity. But the mechanisms we inherited, suitable for the ancestral condition, are the wrong ones for today. The early days of social psychology can help make the dilemma clear.

Social psychology started out as a science more dismal than economics. Solomon Asch (1951) showed that under social pressure a person would claim that two lines of different lengths were the same; Muzafer Sherif (1955) showed that if you divided a group of kids into two groups, they would quickly and intensely dislike each other; Philip Zimbardo (1971) showed how if you created a fictitious prison and assigned students to either a prisoner or a guard role, the guards would become vicious and the prisoners oppressed; Stanley Milgram (1963) showed that with encouragement from an authority figure, one person would electrically shock another into silence. Results of their research were more subtle than that. But, on the whole, their experiments showed us that we weren't the independent, rational, open-minded, noble creatures that we thought we were.

Let's start with the mother of all universal constraint mechanisms. Since your hunting-gathering band is more trustworthy than people in those other bands, and since your fellow band members and leaders confirm through social pressure and authority that your way of doing things is the right way, then the world must be exactly like you and the other band members think it is.

This absolute certainty constrains generativity right at its very heart and soul, because generativity depends on the ability to step back, analyze, recombine old and imagine new parts, and come up with something different. If things are as they should be, why would anyone in their right mind want to change them? Shades of Voltaire. We live in the best of all possible worlds. And that's in part because we've figured out how the world really is, and pretty much everyone in the band agrees.

According to social psychology, people believe, by and large, that their own perspectives aren't perspectives at all. Instead, they believe that they possess an accurate and objective map of reality. A perspective that is different from one's own, then, by definition, is naïve, misguided, a personality problem, delusional, or just plain dumb.

Moskowitz describes this as *the* core problem for social cognition, right in the first chapter of his overview of the field. Most humans, he writes, live in a state of grace that social cognition calls "naïve realism." Gordon Moskowitz defines it as "the belief that our experience of things is one of an objective reality opening itself up to us" (2005, p. 22). According to naïve realism, people don't think they have a perspective linked to reality in some way. They think they have an accurate and complete map of reality, period.

The problem is this: decades of research in social psychology and social cognition show, beyond a shadow of a doubt, that objective reality is never the only thing that any human actually experiences, maybe not even most of it.

Now for a cautionary note worth some emphasis: No one—in the field of social cognition or in this book—is about to go to the other extreme and claim that the world is only a mental construction. Neither Moskowitz nor I nor anyone else with a shred of sense thinks that reality plays no role whatsoever—or, worse, that it doesn't exist. Most of us understand that there's a reality that predates our arrival into a particular task, a reality that will continue long after we've left, whatever changes might have been made to it.

But, as the field of social cognition shows over and over again, humans tend to collapse their perspective *and* reality together and call it *all* objective reality. True, all human knowledge is embedded in a perspective. Buddha and the transcendental phenomenologists disagree, but, with all due respect to followers of the Gautama and Husserl, I think that they've just achieved a higher level of naïve realism. The truths derived from meditating, or from bracketing, as the phenomenologists say, can be powerful indeed. But they always remain, in part, a product of the perspectives from which the meditating or bracketing was launched and to which it must return. A human can't escape it.

Naïve realism is a human universal, the mother of all constraint mechanisms. The hypothesis is that it coevolved with generativity to keep the innovations that analysis and combination made possible coherent enough to form local culture with a small *c*. But there is more to the story of generativity and constraints than the universal human part. The phrase *the Big Bang* calls to mind an explosive moment. But once we turn the photo into a film we will see innovations turn into constraints on further innovation, and we will also see constraints inspire innovations when a particular constraint hinders rather than helps task performance. In other words, the mechanisms work at different levels of scale. The appearance of generativity and constraints in the Culture Big Bang made the mechanisms possible, and then the historical trajectory of different bands applied them iteratively in the details of the tasks that made up lived experience.

Computer Critters Go Hiking

I'd like to show in an abstract way how they work together—generativity and constraints. The computer can serve as a toy for the exercise. John Holland, one of the founders of complexity science, created what he called a *genetic algorithm* to show how the two balance each other out in action, not only as a general theory but also as a practical tool to solve real-world problems (1975/1992).

Here's an example of how Holland's model works. A favorite of the computer modelers is the *knapsack problem*. It caught my attention because of how I felt when I first tried backpacking. Mostly backpacking taught me why god invented burros. But it also made me aware of the problem of getting the most value out of the items that you can jam into a pack. As any backpacker knows, there are other important considerations (especially weight), but this model is based on only size and value.

The knapsack problem goes like this: You have a bunch of things of different sizes and values, and you want to get as much total value out of the full knapsack load as you can. *Value* here means use value—usefulness while you're in the backcountry. A classic "combinatorial optimization" problem, as the computer types call it. Now, how to solve it with algorithms that *constrain* the innovations that might be created.

The problem has to be represented in a computational kind of way. First create a world of computer critters. Imagine them as a bunch of little stick figures on a screen. Give each of them an empty knapsack of the same size. To describe the things that can go into a knapsack, use two numbers, where each pair of numbers tells you the *size* and the *use value* of an object. There are a lot of different kinds of objects, big and worthless, big and valuable, small and valuable, small and worthless, and everything in between those extremes. So we start the computer run with a couple of hundred critters and give each of them some objects that vary randomly in sizes and values. Into the knapsacks the objects go.

That's the first *generative* step. Now we come to the *constraints*. To translate constraints into something the computer can understand, define a *constraint function*, something that says how good or bad each combination of things in the knapsacks in fact is.

Notice here how the generativity/constraint loop is now tied to a task, something we require prior to any discussion of culture with a small *c*. Generativity is innovation to change how some task is done. In this case, the task is backpacking. How do we figure out how to pack the best backpack? How do we tell as we innovate which pack is better than another?

The first thing the constraint will do is check the size limit. A knapsack can only carry up to some maximum total size of items. So, for each critter, the function adds up the total size numbers of all the items in the knapsack. If the size is too big, the function can just let the critter remain but remove items from the knapsack at random until all the items fit.

Now to the *second* part of the constraint function. It sums the use value of all the items that now fit in a critter's knapsack. It turns out that just by chance some knapsacks will have a collection of objects that sum to a higher value than others do. Those critters have a head start in the game, because they're closer to the best possible arrangement that a knapsack can hold. They've lucked into a better knapsack load than the other critters.

Now for a major constraint on what happens next. The critters with higher value knapsacks are more likely to "reproduce" with each other, metaphorically speaking. All critters will be paired with another, the probability skewed by value of what's in the pack. It is the computer scientist's way to apply an evolutionary metaphor to a mechanism of social change.

When they reproduce, two critters will swap some of their own size and value numbers that represent what is in their knapsack. For example, each critter might cut its own list of size/value numbers in half, then give one half to another critter and take half of theirs back in return. Now each critter has a new string of numbers, a new arrangement of items with different sizes and values in its knapsack, and the constraint function starts a new cycle. It checks to make sure each critter's knapsack isn't overloaded, and then it sums up the value of all the things in each knapsack. Some critters will be doing better than they did before, some worse. Then they all pair off and reproduce again, the ones with higher backpack values again tending to pick others with higher backpack values.

If this is starting to sound like the luck of the draw followed by the computer critter equivalent of going to the right schools, that's because that is exactly what is going on. One result of such so-called artificial society models is a rapid increase in disparity of wealth—or, in this case, disparity in value of backpack loads.

So you see how this thing works? Starting from just a random assignment of items to knapsacks, the critters that carry around the higher total value keep reproducing with each other, over and over again. The same *constraints* apply on each cycle—stay within maximum size of the knapsack, and make it more likely that those critters with high total knapsack value trade knapsack items with each other.

Some of the critters will get more and more value out of what's in their knapsacks as time goes on. In the end, the genetic algorithm may not produce the absolutely best possible knapsack arrangement, but it will end up with a few ways to pack a knapsack that are high on the scale of best possible combinations of size and value. It will also end up with a lot of critters who are screwed, low-value critters who keep exchanging in vain. And it will have done it without writing an equation or sitting there for hours trying all the combinations out. And, what's truly amazing, the genetic algorithm will do this in a very brief period of time. It's a simple but powerful example of how, in theory, innovations become constraints that can quickly shape and then just as quickly limit the world.

(See Ross Peterson discussing genetic algorithms at https://www.you tube.com/watch?v=ejxfTy4lI6I, for an example. There are many more of these "artificial society" models on YouTube. Genetic algorithms often have a *mutation* function, where a few parts of the size/value string of numbers change at random for each critter every so often. That opens up possible combinatorial-learning. I won't worry about that part here.)

The computer model *cannot* combinatorial-learn like people can, in the way that Gregory Bateson described with his concept of *deuterolearning* (if you recall the examples in the previous section). The critters can work with the original parts, but they can't consciously invent new ones. Not in this model. The computer doesn't say, "Hey, what if we put a couple of expandable pockets on the outside of the knapsack and some Velcro loops to hang things off the back?" or "What if we thought up a better way to transport these objects, like loading them all onto a drone and the hell with knapsacks?" But, still, the computer helps visualize how constraints balance generative mechanisms and give them direction. Without constraints the generativity would run out of control, like the amplifying loop between a microphone and speaker that produces a screech.

The amazing thing about *Homo sapiens*, with its bigger brain and its language, was that our ancestors could run a program in their imagination without having to do trial and error. As one colleague put it, the mind is a "social simulator." It's not an accident that Ben and Jerry didn't create Liver 'n' Onions ice cream. They didn't need to develop and market it to see whether it would work. They just simulated it with their own internal genetic algorithms, and their flavor-selection function took care of the rest.

So what would a picture of this generative/constraint trade-off look like as it unfolded over time? In the Culture Big Bang, generativity took off and produced a dramatic increase in innovation. So far, so good. That sentence describes the archaeological record starting around fifty thousand years ago. But then things quickly started to stabilize. Ethnic or culture clusters formed, as the archaeologists Klein and Edgar called them in a quote cited earlier, and then those clusters stayed in place long enough to leave a consistent trace. That, too, corresponds with the archaeological record.

Waves of innovation from generativity. Stable patterns based on con-straints. Then innovation to solve a problem that the constraint caused. It turns out that this cycle—change and then stability and then change and then stability, and so on forever—is a cliché in nature, not to mention in social theory. Gabriel Tarde, a founder of sociology, described growth spurts followed by slowdowns in his diffusion theory in the nineteenth century, based on imitation and innovation (described in LaTour, 2005). Even before Tarde, Auguste Comte, another founder, wrote of social statics and social dynamics—he was trying to imitate Newton—and how the two alternated in periods of innovation and stability.

A graph helps visualize the innovation/constraint dynamic over time, a graph of what the mathematicians call a logistic growth or S-curve. Let me show you in figure 1.3 an example from the dozens found on the web. There are dozens because the curve describes so many different phenomena.

This particular example is linked to Everett Rogers's work on diffusion of innovation (2010). A colleague and I used it in previous work on illegal-

The S-shaped diffusion curve and adopter categories

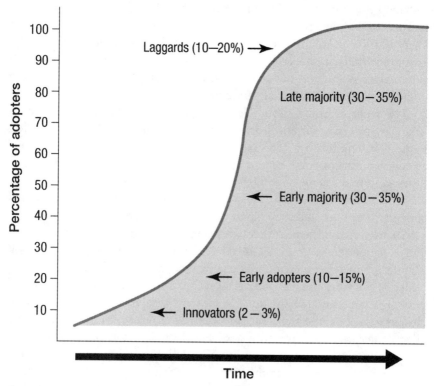

Figure 1.3.
Source: Adapted from Ontario Health Promotion Research Center

drug epidemics (Agar & Reisinger, 2002). The successful ones—though "successful" might be the wrong word for widespread drug dependence—act like this S-curve. In this context, the medical field would call it an *epidemic incidence curve*. But it could represent many other changes, large and small. Apple products often took off like this—the iPhone, for example. Social movements could take off like this—the Tea Party, for instance, or Occupy Wall Street or ISIS. Something doesn't exist, and suddenly it seems like it's everywhere.

Not all innovations diffuse, of course. Most of them probably never make it past that first lower turning point—*inflection point*, they call it—as the curve shifts from a slow rise to exponential growth. And even successful innovations will eventually flatten out—the second inflection point—as the diffusion runs its course after it affects as many in a population as it is going to.

On the most general level, the Culture Big Bang had to have been this kind of change—slow growth off a baseline, a sudden turn upward into an exponential increase driven by generativity, then a flattening out as constraints fence off the limits of the space. The Big Bang metaphor is clear enough from the way the graph explodes upward. But what does that line represent? One way to think about it is that the line represents a rate of innovation—very slow for a very long time, picking up a bit with *Homo erectus* and early *Homo sapiens* (as we'll see in the next chapter on language), then past the first inflection point, and, whoosh, the Culture Big Bang. Then constraints kick in—not only biological selection but also social mechanisms to slow innovations down long enough to try them out, accept or reject them, refine them, teach them, and put them to work. Those social and biological mechanisms formed culture with a small *c*, and there was plenty of room in the space generativity opened up for many different variations.

Small-*c* culture Usually Defined as Constraints

If you look at some of the great definitional moments in culture-with-a-small-*c* research, the emphasis is clearly on this constraint part.

Franz Boas, revered founder of academic American cultural anthropology, got right to the heart of it and used the word *shackles* to describe culture with a small *c* in a spirit close to this book: "In fact, my whole outlook on social life is determined by this question: How can we recognize the shackles that tradition has laid upon us? For when we recognize them, we are also able to break them" (Boas, 1974, p. 42).

Or consider this classic definition, from sociology in 1923: "If men define situations as real, they are real in their consequences" (Thomas & Thomas, 1928, pp. 571–72).

One more example, this one by Ward Goodenough, also often cited and a founder of the field of cognitive anthropology: Culture is "whatever it is one has to know or believe in order to operate in a manner acceptable to its members, and do so in any role that they accept for any one of themselves" (1957, p. 167).

Consider what has to be one of the most frequently cited definitions in the world—that of Clifford Geertz in his book *The Interpretation of Cultures*: "Believing, with Max Weber, that man is an animal suspended in webs of significance he himself has spun, I take culture to be those webs, and the analysis of it to be therefore not an experimental science in search of law but an interpretive one in search of meaning" (1973, p. 5).

"Shackles" is about social constraints, not generativity. So are self-spun "webs," "consequences," and "appropriateness." A culture with a small c may be a beautiful or an ugly thing in the eyes of beholders or outsiders, but it is also a constraint, a limit, that works against generativity. That—so goes the hypothesis here—is exactly what it was designed to do.

Culture with a small c, by these definitions, is more a constraining than a creative force even though it owes its development to the generativity of culture with a capital C. That's what had to happen in the ancestral condition. Evolution would not have been kind to a group of nonstop innovators. Probably, as the Big Bang curve turned upward, some hunting-gathering bands did conduct the experiment, a sort of Upper Paleolithic "let a thousand generativities bloom." Some bands might have generated continuously. They wouldn't have lasted long.

And probably, once *Homo sapiens* started innovating at a rapid pace, other hunting-gathering bands conducted a different experiment. Those bands innovated but then overreacted with constraints and froze those early innovations into place. Too much in the way of constraints. Those bands, too, would probably have lost out in the evolutionary game.

But here's the good news: That ability to analyze and combine didn't disappear as constraints developed. And—one more time, just to be clear— the innovation/constraint dynamic reflected in the S-curve can apply at many different levels of scale. In this book so far, I have introduced it for the Culture Big Bang, the major transition from *Homo erectus* to *Homo sapiens*. But it applies to lower levels of scale as well. For example, I wonder who the first guy or gal was who came up with the idea of making a flute out of a piece of animal bone. I'll bet that person became very popular very quickly. And I'll bet that flutes diffused, first within the band of the innovator, and then with other bands with whom they came into contact. Or maybe most bands had tinkerers to whom the possibility was obvious after the Big Bang and it was a case of independent invention.

The different levels of scale are related, because the highest level is the Big Bang. It made the lower levels of innovations possible, which, in turn, themselves became constraints on further innovation. This is how capital-C culture grew small-c cultures of so many different sorts. And this is why figuring out cultural conflicts requires us to go up in scale until we get to the common humanity, available in the culture with a capital-C Big Bang.

A Minimal Definition of Small-c culture

How can we begin talking about culture with a small c in some sensible way that can handle both the hunting-gathering band of the ancestral condition and the contemporary hodgepodge of cultural hybrids who have to deal with each other in our connected world?

Maybe we should just start with a very narrow and focused question to decide whether we are dealing with something small-c cultural at all. Here's a first try at an answer: If at least two people share a way of doing at least one task together, a way that could in principle be changed, then we could say that those two people share a "culture" for doing that task.

So if you want to call something "cultural," and use it to say that two people share it, you have to see them involved in at least one task together, and you have to be able to show that that way of doing the task could, in principle, be changed. In other words, they're *making sense* to each other in order to get something done, something that could in principle be done differently.

This is a minimal and provisional definition to get this book started. Notice that "culture" doesn't necessarily imply "community" in the sense of a face-to-face small group like hunter-gatherer bands in the ancestral condition. If I meet a stranger about my age who went to Catholic grammar school before the time of Pope John XXIII, we will have several shared ways of making sense of tasks that we were taught by the nuns. It can serve as raw material for an improvisational comedy routine even though we have never met before. This example foreshadows the idea of an *imagined community*, a concept we'll put to work later in this book.

This minimalist definition of culture also works for animals, as it should, given the new attitude in recent animal research. Consider the group of macaques who live on the Japanese island of Koshima (see http://alfre.dk/monkeys-washing-potatoes/ for a brief summary).

Back in the 1950s, researchers began observing the band. The sweet potatoes the monkeys ate sometimes had sand on them. They would just brush it off. Then one day a particular female got the bright idea of washing the sweet potato in the river. She was the first to do this. Her relatives quickly followed suit. The practice diffused, and within a decade every macaque on the island was washing their potatoes. That same clever monkey experimented with dipping the sweet potato in ocean water, which both cleaned and flavored it. That practice, too, diffused rapidly throughout the island. Now, though the original innovator and the original adopters are long gone, washing potatoes in seawater is common practice. It improved the quality of macaque life more than the iPhone did mine.

Does this mean we can talk about a culture of macaques on the island? By my minimalist definition, it does. At least as far as the task of washing the sand off their food goes.

This early research points to another theme that has already appeared in the book. Obviously potato washing isn't on the same level as a coordinated social activity like a mastodon hunt. But it does show that this culture business has a long pedigree that goes further back than the Garden of Eden and well beyond it.

The pedigree, which I only discovered working on this book, was recently the centerpiece of a National Academy of Sciences conference, titled "The Extension of Biology Through Culture" (2016). Here is a summary of the conference theme: "The cultural transmission of behavior and artefacts [provides] not only . . . our own species but also many non-human animals with a 'second inheritance system,' built on the evolutionary foundations of the genetic inheritance system, but extending and interacting with it, in new and significant ways. Research on both human and animal social learning and traditions has burgeoned in recent years with many new and exciting insights and discoveries, often built through new methodological approaches" (National Academy of Sciences, 2016). Apparently dual inheritance theory doesn't just apply to humans.

Still missing—as mentioned earlier—is an equally clear concept of what "language" is all about in the Culture Big Bang story. There will be language with both a capital L and a small l. So we'll take a look at language now and, along the way, slowly begin stirring language and culture together so that we can get to the concept of languaculture.

Language

2

I N THE PREVIOUS CHAPTER, I looked at the dark underbelly of the culture concept. Culture is now pitched in popular discourse as cause of many of our contemporary problems, as well as a source of diversity to cure those problems, and, as a bonus, it can describe and explain almost any problem, especially in the "culture of X" formula, where "X" can be virtually anything or anyone. It reminds me of what the organizational theorists call "the garbage can model," which proposes that an organization "is a collection of choices looking for problems, issues and feelings looking for decision situations in which they might be aired, solutions looking for issues to which they might be the answer, and decision makers looking for work" (Cohen, March, & Olsen, 1972, p. 1).

I was once at a language conference with the late John Gumperz, deity of linguistic anthropology. It was very interdisciplinary. On one occasion, several of his colleagues approached and asked him, "How do you tell which papers are by anthropologists?" "It's easy," John said, "they're the ones who never say the word *culture*."

If it did its job, the previous chapter should have left the reader wondering whether there is any point in saving the concept. Can it handle global society with its hybrid citizens and their fragmented lives? After many years of waffling on my answer to that question, I now think it can. The first step, identified in the previous chapter, was to come up with a definition that ties culture in a more focused way to specific social activities rather than to general and diffuse description and/or explanation of some person or population. For lack of a better term, I used the word *task* for the ground against which the figure of culture must play a role if it's to be of any use today.

The minimal definition of small-*c* culture from the previous chapter: Two or more people share a culture for a single task if they can participate in it together in a way mutually regarded as competent. The maximal definition: The culture of two people is identical if the particular tasks that they competently participate in are identical.

The old-fashioned anthropological idea of a small, isolated village comes close to the maximal definition. It represents a large number of tasks shared—or at least understood—by most all of the villagers. But with this new definition, the concept also includes more limited mixes of people and tasks, like police partners and married couples and a team of carpenters building a house and a group of politicians running for office. And it allows us to see how culture blurs into the rest of the animal kingdom—for example, the potato-washing macaques mentioned earlier.

By this definition, a "culture" can even be more ephemeral than those examples. If I am working in a coffee shop and someone at a nearby table is having a problem with their computer, usually a couple of people will offer to help. The task is to restore the computer to its proper behavior. The shared knowledge and practice comes from the common experience of the people with their laptops. We could go for a poetic metaphor and call it a "firefly" culture. The problem occurs, a few available people familiar with the task connect, they coordinate, the problem usually gets fixed, they disperse, and that particular cultural moment is gone forever.

So, say that any use of the small-*c* culture concept must specify at least one task and at least two people doing it that anchors the concept in lived experience. The concept can be tuned for scope and scale. In the case of my work in a South Indian village long ago, I had to take on a dense network of tasks that pretty much defined cradle-to-grave life for a couple of hundred people. In the case of heroin addicts, it meant adding a few new tasks to life—namely, obtaining and using heroin—that over time came to override and dominate other tasks in that life as addiction set in. For a project that I did for an outpatient cancer clinic, the task was more focused—namely, the task of getting the chemo "cocktail" inside the patient.

We have a lot more work to do to clear up the culture concept and make it useful. The task focus with which the previous chapter ended is just a start. But, for now, we can say that if someone mentions culture, one asks, "What task(s) is this about?" Show me, don't tell me. No task in view, no mention of culture, please, because we won't know what you're talking about in terms of the lived experience of the people involved in it.

The next step for this book is to take a look at something that this focus on tasks forces us to notice. The people doing the tasks of interest, and the people who want to talk about what those people are doing—we are looking at *talking apes*, to borrow the title of Robbins Burling's book about the evolution of language (2005). The small-*c* culture is whatever it is that a newcomer to the task learns to be able to do it. Doing the task involves cooperation and coordination. A proposed innovation in the task may or may not diffuse—that is, be adopted by others as a change in how to perform that task.

Learning, coordination, task innovation, diffusion—these all require some kind of communication. Would human language have offered a leg up in innovation, in diffusion, on learning and on coordination? Would Culture with a capital *C* and—we might as well maintain the parallel for the moment—Language with a capital *L* have interacted in a positive feedback loop that shot the Culture Big Bang S-curve into exponential overdrive? And would language with a small *l* interact with culture with a small *c* to turn innovations into local constraints?

Language? It's as Bad as Culture

"Language," like culture, is another vague and ambiguous concept. Bees have a language, the famous dance to tell other bees the direction and distance to food, don't they? Vervet monkeys have one call for trouble on the ground and another for trouble from the air. Isn't that a language? Well, yes to both—not in the sense of "human speech" but in the broader sense of "communication." But in those two cases—bees and vervet monkeys—the languages are very limited in what they can do. They're pretty much the same everywhere for those particular species, in nature, until human trainers start messing with them. They don't change.

However, the last couple of decades of comparative animal-communication research have been full of surprises. Mostly there have been surprises because of the long-standing arrogant belief of humans that animals are deficient, without thoughts or feelings or any abilities even remotely close to what we humans can do.

The old idea: There is a great chain of being with humans as the top link, subordinated only to god, who in turn instructs the humans immediately below him to make use of the subhuman beasts and plants and prosper. Animals have no language, no thoughts, no emotions, no culture. Comparative animal research shows how embarrassing and anthropocentric and just plain naïve this view was.

Decades ago my graduate advisor told me that he had given a lecture on how animals could not communicate negation. A student wrote a final paper about her dog to give the prof some grief. Whenever she came home, and the dog was over the top with affection and playfulness, she knew that some dog-caused catastrophe had occurred during the day while she was at school. The dog was a liar: "Who, me?" Her paper was an essay for an undergraduate class, not a journal article. But still . . . Even way back then, there were rumblings of animal intelligence in the ether. Now we know from animal research that several species engage in deception.

Alex the parrot and Kanzi the bonobo and Chaser the dog and the New Caledonian crows can do things that the beasts beneath us were never supposed to be capable of. The one clear and unique human specialty lies in vocalization (Fitch, 2010). With the emergence of *Homo sapiens*, new neurological wiring evolved to connect the neocortex and the vocal tract. This enabled the controlled production of discrete sound units, independent of anything the sounds might mean, though, even here, some species of birds also have a version of brain-vocal pathways that allow them to have dialects. Sort of a capital-*S* Song and small-*s* song. As I write this, there are arguments about the Neanderthals, some primates, and marine mammals, indicating the capacity for more control over sound production than was previously believed. There are also arguments about whether the basic human sound unit is a single sound or a syllable and whether the original motive for use was speech or song. For my purposes here it doesn't matter.

The point is that we are now in the land of what the linguists call *duality of patterning*, a concept introduced by Charles Hockett to distinguish human from animal communication (1960). Suddenly, as measured by the evolutionary clock, humans controlled a signaling system of many separate pieces that had no necessary ties to the meanings they conveyed. This biological innovation led to a combinatorial explosion in the number of discrete, arbitrary signals that could be sent through the vocal-auditory channel. With this combinatorial explosion, generativity enters into communication in a major way. We will return to the concept of duality of patterning later in this chapter.

In fact, one view of human language now—given what we've learned from recent animal and brain research—is that it's kind of a Rube Goldberg machine tinkered together by evolution out of parts already available to many of our human predecessors and animal contemporaries. The biological pieces involved in language do many other things and did so before *Homo sapiens*. And, though humans can communicate much more elaborately than other animals, most of the biological pieces by which they accomplish it can be found in more rudimentary form among our mammalian relatives.

The new sound system that suddenly appeared not only allowed *Homo sapiens* to communicate with a very large number of spoken words but also explains both the achievements and the limits of what our primate relatives can do when we humans try and teach them to talk with us. Other primates don't have the neurological wiring or the vocal equipment to speak using a large number of discrete but meaningless sound units.

Once the researchers gave up on teaching animals how to talk and switched to a form of communication based on sign language or computer symbols, our primate cousins did much better, as long as humans taught them. You sometimes read or hear from humans that, once primates are given some way to express themselves that doesn't rely on speech, it's like dealing with a two-year-old human, not a mindless, soulless, unfeeling creature unrelated to us. It's an interesting comment, since human language learning takes off at around two years of age.

Language and Culture, Capital and Small

Human language appeared with the Culture Big Bang for a lot of plausible reasons, as described by the experts in the field (see, for example, Burling, 2005). But I don't think the experts noticed that language has characteristics that make it the perfect vehicle for analysis and combination, the heart of *generativity*. And once that ability is filled in to make a specific language, its social nature and the way it carves pathways of habitual thought and action also make it a *constraint*, something that sets limits on what can be said given what has been said before. It may well have been written at many times in places I just haven't discovered, but it does look like language served as *both* a generative *and* a constraint mechanism, *at the same time*, just like culture did. So, as with the culture concept, we get Language with a capital *L* and language with a small *l*—language as a *universal* human ability and language as a means of communication for a *specific* group of people.

I'm going to use *language* for the rest of the book to mean "spoken human language." Most everyone speculates that language appeared with the Culture Big Bang. But most everyone also agrees—now—that we humans have had a bad habit of overstating the differences between animal/early human communication and language. The transition was more continuous than we used to think. In fact, animals have capabilities that we used to claim were exclusively human, including *culture* itself. The potato-washing innovation among the macaques in Japan mentioned in the last chapter is one classic example of a local primate culture with a small *c*, however basic it might have been. Primates trained to use non-vocal symbols are just another example of abilities among animals that we humans hadn't imagined possible.

But the difference between them and us—between our nearest living relatives, chimps and bonobos, and modern *Homo sapiens*—it remains substantial. Let me start with language with a small *l*. In the ancestral condition, languages with a small *l* and cultures with a small *c* developed together. Language and tasks, so goes the hypothesis, grew out of people doing things together and communicating with each other while they were doing them, and later telling stories about how things were done and teaching others how to do them.

Robot Talkers

Luc Steels builds robots to show how language can arise out of interaction in a particular task (2001). (See Luc Steels's talk "Can Robots Invent Their Own Language?" at https://www.youtube.com/watch?v=AaVnyn1tSIE, for a brief video from 2015.) He calls his research *language games* to honor the concept of the same name in the philosophy of Ludwig Wittgenstein. Steels designed two robots that create shared concepts to communicate about some part of a situation they're both in. It is beyond the scope of this chapter to review the robot computer model in detail. Besides, they aren't exactly discussing the meaning of life. But the robots do get pretty good at what he calls "the guessing game."

The guessing game demonstrates how the robots integrate models, sensory and motor hardware, communication, and the details of a shared environment. The *speaker* robot calls the *listener* robot's attention to some object in their shared space, which the speaker then conceptualizes and communicates with some symbol. The listener robot looks for something similar in its own models. If it doesn't find anything, it begins a process of learning a new concept that it didn't have before. If it does have a related model, then it makes a guess as to just what object in the environment the speaker robot referred to. The robots go back and forth until, whatever their differences might be in terms of how models and symbols are organized, they finally agree that, with a particular symbol, they are talking about the same thing.

The two robots build a culture with a small *c* around a task by means of created symbols. And what they build both limits what the next symbol might mean and makes it easier to figure out, since they are more constrained by what they have already jointly built. Language tied to a shared task, and the growth of a shared symbolic vocabulary based on that task, produces a local culture with a small *c* and a local language with a small *l* at the same time.

Language with a small *l and* culture with a small *c* coevolve with shared-task activities, an argument based on the fact that language and experience are part and parcel of the same flow of human life. There is no language apart from *context*, not in the real world. Ludwig Wittgenstein, the inspiration for Luc Steels's robots, wrote that long ago in *Philosophical Investigations*. So did Bronisław Malinowski, a founder of linguistic anthropology. So did the American pragmatists, like William James. Language, they all said, is how it is *used* by its speakers and hearers, not how its grammar is formally described by linguists. Language and culture become part of the same phenomenon. It's not a matter of studying them separately and then later figuring out the relationship between the two. It's a matter of studying both at the same time.

Merlin Donald makes the same point in his book on the evolution of cognition, *Origins of the Modern Mind*, only he uses the concept of *mental model* to foreground the link between language, culture, and task (1993). Mental model is something that a person makes up to understand what another person means and figure out how to respond to them. One way of thinking about culture with a small *c* is to think of it as shared mental models linked to the same task, but that is too simple; even soul mates have some differences in their mental models. Besides, people can do tasks together (the shared part), though their purposes—and the models they are tied to—can be wildly different. As in the saying, politics makes for strange bedfellows.

But if we stay focused on a particular task and the people involved in it, then something shared has to be at work. What is said and done has to make sense to the other participants who are talking and listening and doing. A task-based mental model, for humans as well as for robots, is a name Donald uses for that unspoken social glue that holds language and thought and action together for those engaged in it. Long ago Michael Polanyi called it *tacit knowledge* (1958/1962).

In his book, Donald refers to an amusing example from Philip Johnson-Laird's work on mental models: One person says to another, "The ham sandwich is sitting at table number 5 and getting impatient" (cited in Donald, 1993, p. 229). A traditional linguistic analysis would foreground a contradiction. The grammar says that inanimate objects like sandwiches don't *sit at a table* or *feel* anything. The mental model, however, would be much more useful. It will tell you, the eavesdropper at table number 6, that you are in a restaurant and a waitperson is talking to the cook. The ham sandwich refers to a person at a particular table—namely, table number 5—who ordered one and hasn't received it yet. The sentence, heard as part of the *task* of working in a restaurant by two of its participants, makes perfect sense.

Language and task are woven together, and the task from which the language emerges and to which it applies produces a micro-culture with a small *c*, shared by waitperson and cook. Both of them learned a system of table numbering and a convention of referring to customers by what they order. This matters for where this book is going, because specific task-based communication will be where culture with a small *c* can be rescued from the ancestral condition and updated for our global world. When two mental models working away in the tacit background suddenly fall out of sync and disrupt the task flow, the abstract cultural diversity problem comes to life. And it is here that it has to be handled.

Here's another funny example that just happened while I was working on this chapter: I was in the checkout line at the neighborhood supermarket. A middle-aged woman was at the cash register, and a teenage girl was bagging items. As I stepped up for my turn at checkout, the middle-aged woman asked me, "Plastic or paper?" (referring to my preference for the kind of bag I wanted my purchase placed in). Before I could say a word, the teenage girl said, "Hey, that's a *bagger* question, not a *checker* question." I chuckled, but she was visibly annoyed. Without my mental model of the supermarket and the cast of characters and their tasks, the assertion and the annoyance would have made no sense at all. Without her comment, I wouldn't have realized that the mental models in play were different in ways that produced conflict within the task.

The examples of the restaurant and the supermarket show how language with a small *l* works as a *constraint* for particular tasks. Consider the ancestral condition again: Those clusters of tasks and symbols and mental models socialize a child into a certain way of being and doing. They create out-of-awareness and deeply embedded habitual patterns of thought and action. They locate a person in the small social world of the hunting-gathering band. They wrap a person in an identity whose loss would put the odds of survival very low. That local configuration of culture with a small *c* and language with a small *l* defines who a person is with reference to a particular task and to the other people engaged with it.

Linguistic anthropologists, including this one, see language with a small *l* and culture with a small *c* as going together like bread and butter, or ham and eggs, or—given how peculiar ethnographers look to locals as we stumble around in a community trying to learn what's what—like Laurel and Hardy. Linguistic anthropology is founded on a simple premise—for an outsider, those publicly available sounds are an inroad into a different culture. But to get to the culture part, you have to figure out what those sounds *mean*.

In the previous chapter, several definitions of culture were quoted to show how researchers emphasized the conservative, constraining nature of culture with a small *c*. Is there something similar in linguistics? Yes, there is. The famous Sapir-Whorf hypothesis, a core component of linguistic anthropology, argued decades ago that language was a major constraint on thought and action. A long list of German philosophers said the same thing before that. A couple of quotes will lay the hypothesis out in the words of its creators.

Whorf first:

> We dissect nature along lines laid down by our native language. The categories and types that we isolate from the world of phenomena we do not find there because they stare every observer in the face; on the contrary, the world is presented in a kaleidoscopic flux of impressions which has to be organized by our minds—and this means largely by the linguistic systems in our minds. (1956, p. 213)

And here's one way that Sapir wrote it:

> Human beings do not live in the objective world alone, nor alone in the world of social activity as ordinarily understood, but are very much at the mercy of the particular language which has become the medium of expression for their society. . . . The worlds in which different societies live are distinct worlds, not merely the same world with different labels attached. . . . Even comparatively simple acts of perception are very much more at the mercy of the social patterns called words than we might suppose. . . . We see and hear and otherwise experience very largely as we do because the language habits of our community predispose certain choices of interpretation. (in Mandelbaum, 1958, p. 69)

The Sapir-Whorf hypothesis is controversial today. The controversy is very much about the difference between Language with a capital *L* and language with a small *l*. Mainstream linguistics now sees language as a human universal. Linguistics in service of understanding a particular human group sees language as historically shaped by that group. In fact, both things are true, and we'll put them together into the same framework later in the book. For the moment, the idea that a particular language constrains perception, interpretation, and subsequent action is obvious. How do you think lawyers, advertising copywriters, and Washington spin doctors make a living? Not to mention fiction authors and poets? Language with a small *l* and culture with a small *c*, linked in mutually reinforcing ways in the context of tasks, constrain individual mental models via socially shared mechanisms.

A child learns a language, and an adult uses it in tasks, over and over again in everyday life. It is a social flywheel. It evens out the generative bursts of any single person or group. It places them under community control through symbolic means. To depart from the collective language is to become an individual who makes no sense, has no role, and is incapable of participation in shared tasks—in other words, a human who is not a social person at all.

Without constraints, the new generativity would have been doomed to be a flash in the proverbial pan. Innovation would have flared brightly in evolutionary history and then consumed itself as it went into exponential overdrive. Something had to flatten that logistic growth curve out. But the very constraints that developed to balance it out—culture with a small *c* and language with a small *l*—are now a major source of problems in the brave new world that those new abilities have created.

Homo Erectus Were Good Mimes

The experts say that human thought and language showed signs of life well before *Homo sapiens* launched into the Culture Big Bang. Donald, whose book informs some of the previous section, says that "language, including speech, had started to evolve much earlier than 50,000 years ago" (1993, p. 203).

Donald speculates that a *middle stage* between early hominins and the Big Bang might fill in the gap. He speculates for several reasons. First of all, *Homo erectus*, the ancestor to modern humans, must have been capable of some communication that went beyond animal systems. Their brain size increased considerably, up to 80 percent of later *Homo sapiens'* volume. They migrated out of Africa and populated Europe and Asia, and they dealt with harsh and changing climates. They used fire and cooked food and developed new tool kits. *Homo erectus* didn't change much over their long run, from about one and a half million to two hundred thousand years ago. But still, they must have developed beyond the abilities of the primates and the first hominins. *Homo erectus* sounds like a good candidate for the slow-growth part of the Big Bang curve before the takeoff point.

They probably didn't invent the pluperfect subjunctive, but they must have had a more sophisticated communication system than the chimps did.

Donald's second argument for prelinguistic sophistication involves contemporary examples. Prelinguistic children, illiterate deaf-mutes (to use Donald's terminology), and some famous clinical cases also have no language, but they are capable of plenty of communication. Besides, even for humans with language, skills like art, music, sports, and crafts are learned in part without it. And consider games like charades where communication without language is the point of it all. Examples like these, says Donald, suggest mental and communication abilities that predate language. Mimetic culture, he thinks, was a system of communication that went beyond the moment and set up conditions for human language.

Mimetic culture—*mime* being the hint of what is to come—has its roots in *episodic* memory, an ability that animals have. Remember the stories of Waldo the cat? He was more than just a reaction to a can opener. But he certainly was that as well, and a reaction to a can opener is a perfect example of episodic memory. Such memories activate when a simple cue, or a few of them, actually occur in the world and register on the animal's sense receptors. There is a direct link between perception and episodic memory and action. But there is no sense of a self separate from the episode, nor is there much (if any) remembering or imagining of the episode absent the cues that actually trigger it.

Mimetic culture is what Donald thinks happened between those episodic abilities widely found in the animal kingdom and the later arrival of human language. A major achievement of mimetic culture—when compared to episodic memory—was what he called *autocueing*, which means that a memory could be called up and communicated separately from when the task itself actually occurred.

Mimetic culture probably relied on iconic signs. *Iconic* means a sign that has some kind of resemblance to what it refers to. One can communicate without the object or person or event actually being present. Flapping your arms suggests a bird. A ritual dance suggests a hunt because one dancer wears an animal skin and another carries a weapon. A throwing motion with an empty hand suggests an actual toss of a spear. Most readers will have seen a mime perform, like the famous Marcel Marceau, a master of iconic signs. If Waldo had come up to me, looked me in the eye, and imitated the sound of a can opener while rotating his teeth in a circular motion, he would have been mimetic.

A second change with mimetic culture, according to Donald, was a shift away from what he calls *cognitive egocentricity*—in other words, an ability to think of a task separate from one's own doing of it. This ability was the beginning of a sense of self separate from immediate experience. This sense of self was crucial in the eventual development of human language. One can't talk *about* the world in generative mode unless one stands *apart* from it.

Both developments (autocueing and a separate sense of self) distinguished mimetic culture from the episodic culture of animals and early hominins. Or so Donald argues. Both developments would also have been critical steps along the path to the generative ability that drove the Culture Big Bang. Analyzing a whole into parts requires stepping back and looking at it, and exploring combinatorial possibilities requires calling actions to mind separate from when they actually happened. According to Donald, these abilities were present before language developed.

I think Donald's speculation makes a lot of sense. Human language didn't come from nowhere. And, as Donald argues, modern humans still use episodic and mimetic skills. They are part and parcel of our inheritance from animals and early humans.

Mimetic culture names the development of increasingly sophisticated mental models coevolving with increasingly sophisticated abilities to communicate. Mental models, communication systems, task performance, and cultures with a small c *coevolved* in a network of amplifying feedback loops. In retrospect we can see it coming—or think we can—as primates led to early humans led to *Homo sapiens*. Increasing sophistication in one part of the loop led to increasing sophistication in another part led to increasing sophistication in . . . etc., etc., etc. Then, boom, the takeoff into the Culture Big Bang. At least, that is the argument that Donald makes.

Language with a Capital *L*

The preceding sections started with language with a small *l* and how it might have developed along with culture with a small *c*. Along the way, we've slid into capital *C* and *L*. Soon we can lose the artificial separation between culture and language. I had to use this distinction to start the book because of the way most people, including most social scientists and some anthropologists, think about language and culture as separate phenomena.

Now I want to continue with the Culture Big Bang and consider Language with a capital *L*, language as a general human ability rather than a specific language, grounded in tasks, spoken by a particular group of speakers. I want to argue that language and the new generativity, Culture with a capital *C*, were a match made in heaven.

Recall that the new human language relied on sounds that have no necessary relationship to what they mean. *Cat*, to continue to honor the late Waldo, has no necessary relationship to the animal that the sound refers to. The sound sequence does not *resemble* it in some way, so it is not mimetic. It is an arbitrary string of sounds that mean nothing linked with something in the world that means much. Independent sound production gives language its spectacular power to represent and communicate virtually an infinite number of meanings.

Where did this ability come from? Many are the arguments and speculations. The development of Broca's and Wernicke's areas in the brain played a role, as did the enlargement of the brain more generally. Recent research shows "homologues" to those areas in primates. The L-shaped vocal tract, so goes another argument, gradually evolved starting way back in time with bipedalism. Speculation now flourishes that mutation in the FOXP2 gene may have something to do with it, though the jury's still out on that one. As one would expect, whatever the story was, it was made up of many complicated interacting factors. In this business there are no simple causes.

One thing is clear, though, at least as of today: The descent of the larynx—the phrase sounds like a combination of a sci-fi thriller and a gothic computer game—played a crucial role. Like everything else in human evolution, that assertion is no longer the simple fact it used to be. But the lowered larynx allowed humans to produce a virtually infinite number of symbols by stringing together relatively few distinct sounds in multiple ways (Lieberman, 1991). The descended larynx enabled the symbolic combinatorial explosion that interacted with the development of a neocortical–vocal tract connection that made brain control of sound production possible.

But now come the complications. Early modern humans actually appeared roughly one hundred fifty thousand years before the Culture Big Bang took off. Those early modern humans *also* had a descended larynx, according to evidence from skull remains. So why didn't they produce language? Just to complicate things a little more, adult deer and some marine mammals also have a descended larynx.

For now I'll ignore those complications. The evolution of the vocal tract combined with the wiring between it and the neocortex was unique to humans, that much is clear, at least today, at least given what I've read so far. No longer did particular sounds have a particular meaning, like an alarm cry always and only meaning danger. Now sounds coupled with meanings in an arbitrary way. *Arbitrary*, in fact, is another so-called design *feature* of human language, proposed by the same Charles Hockett mentioned earlier who introduced the idea of duality of patterning (1960). Two independent patterns, one made of sound units, the other made of meaning, linked together in an arbitrary way into an extremely large number of meaningful symbols.

And the new symbolic system could represent a task separate from when it actually happened. Hockett called this design feature *displacement*—that language can represent events distant in space and time—a logical choice, since "displace" is about moving a representation to time/space coordinates separate from when the thing represented actually occurred. Language could also slice and dice any task into finer parts and create a representation of them. This feature is called *productivity*. Productivity means language can create new symbols as the need arises.

Hockett argued that duality of patterning, displacement, arbitrariness, and productivity were the four features that best distinguished human language from other communication systems in nature. Notice how well these features also describe what a generative symbolic system might look like, a system helpful to humans trying to analyze and recombine different parts of a task.

Remember when Corballis's concept of generativity was first introduced in the previous chapter? Tasks, the context and the motivation for the new linguistic ability, are all about a body interacting with a world. Doing and talking developed in the context of tasks, just like Luc Steels showed in simplified form with his French robots. The fact that they could develop at all is the capital *C* and *L*; what they turned into over time in different hunting-gathering bands was the small *c* and *l*.

Grammar and Task

Let me describe a few of many other features of Language with a capital *L* to show how well it can work with generativity. Innovation involves human agents engaged in tasks with other agents and objects. A *subject* dealing with an *object* while doing a *task* maps onto the universal Subject/Verb/Object structure of sentence grammar. The structure can have different orders in different languages—Subject/Object/Verb is another common one, familiar to victims of German. But those three pieces will always be there for the transitive verbs—S and V and O, as the linguists abbreviate them—in any human language.

Years ago the literary critic Kenneth Burke argued that a sentence could be understood as the title of a situation (1966). A "summary" would be another way to think about it. Burke's approach to language had the same orientation as an analytic and combinatorial approach to a task. To tell a story—a sequence of sentences organized in a particular way—an experience needed to be broken into parts and (re)arranged. It has to involve actors and actions in some world of objects. The simplest level of organization where that kind of meaning gets communicated in language, he wrote, is at the level of the sentence.

One particular sentence grammar is especially well suited to analyze and recombine parts of a task. It was always my favorite, starting in graduate school days when it was first created, and I'm just understanding why decades later. The theory began with Charles Fillmore's *case grammar*, later called *frame semantics*, continuing today as part of what is called *cognitive grammar* (1968).

For present purposes, Fillmore's original theory is the most straightforward example. It slices and dices tasks and assembles the parts into sentences, along the lines that generativity requires. The grammar is built on the *case relations* that different nouns have to a verb. Here is a sample of the cases he described: *agent* (the active performer of the action); *instrument* (the means by which the action was accomplished); *dative* (the entity affected); *object* (sometimes called *patient*, the target of the action); *factitive* (the result of the action); and *locative* (the place where the action occurred). That's not an exhaustive list, and it gets added to in different ways by different linguists, but it gives a sense of how the grammar works.

Here's a sentence: "Chuck hunted a mastodon behind the mountain with a spear." The fact that this particular *Homo sapiens* was named Chuck means he was probably white. An agent, *Chuck*; an object, *the mastodon*; an instrument, *the spear*; and a location, *behind the mountain*. We also have a verb, *hunt*, and a tense, *past*, that displaces the action in the sentence to a time prior to when it was actually said.

In case grammar, the *verb* is central. At the level of experience, we can translate that to mean that the *task* is central. Each verb carries a *case frame* that shows which cases are necessary and which are optional. For present purposes, notice that the kinds of things that are called *cases* are also the kinds of things people would notice when they analyzed a task—who did it, what was it done on, what do you do it with, where was it done, and so on. Case grammar isn't a bad guide for journalists, either, like the old traditional "who, what, when, where, why, and how."

A case frame can get filled in a lot of different ways. For example: I cut the wood with a [knife, hacksaw, rock, chain saw . . .]. There can be new things that a person might imagine *could* fill the slot. I cut the wood with: A piece of broken glass? A chunk of scrap metal? A trained beaver? Playing with a verb and its cases in language makes combinatorial-learning a distinct possibility. That kind of learning, if you recall from earlier parts of this book, meant that humans didn't just recombine the parts they came up with via analysis. They also imagined new possibilities that weren't part of the original task and put those new parts into the recombination mechanism as well.

Language with a capital *L* interacted with Culture with a capital *C* and its mechanisms for analysis and (re)combination. Generativity and capital-*L* Language mutually amplified each other, the kind of amplification that helped create the Culture Big Bang.

The Culture Big Bang developed across many human sites at roughly the same time, and Language with a capital *L* must have been part of its dramatic takeoff. At the same time, small-*l* language was also part of the story of culture with a small *c*. It emerged in interaction with tasks and mental models for those tasks performed by different hunting-gathering bands as they set off on their own peculiar histories. Those developments produced the small-*c* culture and small-*l* language—the dampening feedback that slowed the generative growth curve down and constrained subsequent innovation.

When we view language like this, it doesn't look like the all-powerful *unique* cause for the Culture Big Bang that it is often described to be. Instead, its power came from its fit with many other evolutionary and historical forces also in play and its ability to interact with—not *cause* but *interact with*—those forces to coproduce that logistic growth curve of the Culture Big Bang. And two of the main forces it interacted with were the generative ability of our ancestors and the development of constraint mechanisms to keep the innovative explosion in check.

That was the power of language in the Culture Big Bang. Language, like culture, worked at *both* inflection points, the first where the curve took off (the analysis and (re)combination of generativity) and the second where it flattened out (the constraints, both universal and those generated by culture with a small *c* and language with a small *l*).

Language was key in the story of the Culture Big Bang, as anthropologists and others have always argued, since it worked with culture, with a capital *C* and with a small *c*, to both enable and constrain the generative leaps that made us what we are today, for better or for worse.

There are, needless to say, other theories on how and why language evolved than just the one I'm arguing in this book. I'm using this theory here because it fits the concept of *languaculture* rather than maintaining the artificial separation between language and culture. The two, as I wrote earlier, are part of the same phenomenon, not parts to be studied separately and later correlated in some way.

The concept will also—this is a preview of material to come—let us eventually get rid of the capital and small language and culture rhetoric. Any effort to handle "cultural problems" requires a blend of what is universally true and what is true only of the local moment. More later.

The first order of business: We need a framework that shows where culture is in language and where language is in culture to understand what languaculture is supposed to mean.

The Rise of the Symbol

Language use has several moving parts. One of the main parts is a *code*. Something happens that can be perceived, and it means something more than just the fact that it occurred. A code is just shorthand for a road map between perception and meaning and meaning and action. Bees have a code to link what they see in the world with their dance in the hive. But it is the same bee code everywhere. Bees don't have duality of patterning. A particular kind of dance always means the same thing. Humans have a code, but it's different from one group to another. The field of *semiotics* can help straighten out this languaculture business. The question is: Where in the code is the culture? Answer: It all starts with duality of patterning.

A "sign" is an element of the code, something that means something to a human who encounters it—I'll stick with humans for the moment. An "encounter" means the human perceived something, called the "signifier." What it meant to the human is called the "signified."

Different kinds of glue can hold signifier to signified. One simple typology by Charles Peirce goes like this:

1. An "indexical" sign works because a piece of a pattern means the presence of the entire pattern. "Where there's smoke, there's fire"—that sort of thing. Think *metonymy*.
2. An "iconic" sign—the kind that Donald argued rose to prominence in mimetic culture—works by resemblance between the signifier and the signified. The sign on my computer screen for the calendar is actually a small icon—it's the same word in computer jargon— that looks like a calendar. Think *metaphor*.
3. With the third type of sign, the glue is neither pattern nor resemblance. It is *arbitrary*—remember, one of the design features of

human language. In other words, there is no necessary reason why a particular signifier should mean a particular signified. There is no reason why the sound *dog* and the sound *cat* should differentiate between an animal that has a master and another that has a staff. It is a matter of convention, something that has to be learned. This kind of sign is called a "symbol."

See the online *Stanford Encyclopedia of Philosophy*, "Pierce's Theory of Signs," for a more complete discussion (Atkin, 2013).

Symbols are where duality of patterning really shines, where the evolution of that neocortex–vocal tract connection really did enable a proliferation of them. The sound system and the meaning system operate independently of each other. Need a new signifier? Create one with a sound system, and assign it arbitrarily to the new meaning. You just created a new piece of language—or, rather, proposed it, because obviously the other people in your world have to accept it as well. Remember Luc Steels's robots?

Think "word" for a moment. Human words, for the most part, are symbols. Not always though. The word *buzz* suggests the sound a bee makes, an example of onomatopoeia or sound symbolism.

Kanzi the bonobo and Chaser the dog learned arbitrary symbols from humans—hundreds of them. They were good at comprehension but not at production, of course, because they don't have the vocal/brain apparatus of humans. They can't talk, but they can listen. Kanzi can also use symbols to communicate with humans, signifiers arbitrarily linked to their signifieds, like plastic chips or computer images. Some of them, I suspect, may be icon- or index-like. But, once learned, the glue that holds the symbol together is fixed. Kanzi can't decompose the chip and make a different kind of chip out of the parts, but he can do some creative word making. For instance, he had trouble chewing kale, so he combined symbols to call it "slow lettuce."

Thanks to neocortical control over the vocal system that developed for *Homo sapiens*, a combinatorial explosion occurred in the signifier system. The symbol is no longer an indivisible whole. A signifier is made up of parts that can be combined and recombined in many different ways to mean different things. The sky is the limit.

Even here, animal research shows that we are not completely unique. If we jump out of mammals via the higher vertebrate category and drop down into birds, we find a case of convergent evolution. Some birds also have a neural-vocal link that allows them to learn new expressions from their parents after birth. In fact some birds, like all human children, won't learn local vocalizations unless they are born into an environment with adults who stimulate their own development. There are bird dialects.

Alex the talking parrot—who had the vocal system that Kanzi would die for—combined parts of two signifiers to make a new one. When given an apple, he called it a *banerry*, according to his trainer, because it tasted like a banana and looked like a cherry. He also called cake *yumbread* from his prior words "yummy" and "bread." Not duality of patterning, but not bad for a birdbrain, as she affectionately called him.

None of this means that in the near future your pet will greet you at the door and ask, "How was your day?" He'll never have the vocal tract to do that. The house robot might, but not your Irish setter. It does mean that, once I learned something about recent animal-communication research, human language, like human culture, looks more like a logical development rather than a sudden miracle.

The question is: How and where and in what way did language and culture mix together as collaborators in the major Culture Big Bang transition?

Languaculture

I'm going to use *languaculture* instead of *language and culture* separately for the rest of the book. It's a term that I borrowed and modified from the work of Paul Friedrich (1989). It fits the flow of recent work that language and culture were part of the same system that made possible the emergence of *Homo sapiens*.

The connection between brain and larynx is the current nominee for the part of languaculture that is most unique to humans when compared to other primates. It is the crucial biological foundation that enables languaculture to be so generative and dynamic. A small number of sounds can be combined and recombined into a virtually infinite number of signifiers. It is, as near as I can tell, the only absolute biological boundary marker between modern humans and the other primates, as far as language and communication go.

Crucial as this combinatorial explosion was for the Culture Big Bang, variations in sounds from one group to another remain limited by the structure of the vocal tract. The ironic conclusion? Even with a sound system that made a combinatorial explosion possible, there are still limited possibilities for variation in phonology among languages.

I first learned this when I explored phonetic transcription. I found a short course that taught how to transcribe not only the sounds of my own language but also other possible sounds that people might use in other languages. The exercise had its exotic moments for an English speaker. For example, do you know what a voiceless lateral fricative is? Make an "L" sound. Now leave your tongue in place more or less—tighten it up a bit to impede air flow—and just breathe out continuously. Never heard of it? You won't be able to learn Navajo—and other languages—without mastering it.

Nevertheless, phonology shows that there are only a comparatively limited number of sounds that we humans can produce, even though the number of words we can produce with that limited number of sounds is very large. Don't get me wrong here—there are ways that phonology alone can be cultural. Stacks of articles describe language and dialect stereotyping, for example. Several colleagues my age told me stories about how they worked to eliminate their Southern accents before they finished graduate school and started interviews for faculty positions in other parts of the country. Why? Because of prejudices back then against a Southern accent. And poetry uses the sound system to meaningful effect. But aside from a few examples like these, there just isn't that much culture in the vocal tract. It is part of languaculture, but it isn't very cultural.

The next level is morphology and syntax, word making and sentence making, more or less. The two are tied together, since in many languages, for example, nouns and verbs are conjugated and declined with grammatical morphemes to show their role vis-à-vis other words in the sentence. There are many variations from one languaculture to another. At the same time, these two levels of languaculture are also fairly restricted spaces, one of the reasons that many linguists argue that grammar is a biologically based human universal. In the view of those linguists, grammars represent a few variations on human universal possibilities.

There are, of course, differences. Spanish uses a no-fault reflexive where some bad thing that you do just happens to you rather than you causing it. Kanarese hangs all kinds of preposition-like morphemes on the verb. German frequently uses directional particles for space and time— sometimes for literal movement, sometimes in a metaphorical way.

But once you learn a second language, you figure out that, whatever the language, certain things need to get done to make words and sentences, and any grammar that you look at will allow you to do most of those things in one way or another. They also make it easier to do a few things rather than others. And if you learn how a second language works grammatically in detail, you know a lot about what to expect when you start to learn another.

It doesn't look like there's a huge amount of culture in morphology and syntax, either, though there are some famous counterexamples. Around the Pacific Rim, for example, several languages have what are called "numeral classifiers." This little devil is a morpheme that hangs on the end of a number. It changes depending on what it is you are counting. So, to take a hypothetical example, the two in "two humans" and the two in "two soccer balls" would look different because the number is being used to count different kinds of things.

At this point the Sapir-Whorf hypothesis calls out for another visit. Whorf, after all, used Hopi grammar, as well as vocabulary, to argue for *linguistic relativism*. He tried to show that Hopi was a timeless language—so much for present, past, and future tense—though later work by his critics argues that it's a matter of an outsider's interpretation, that it was possible to see a grammatical tense system operating in the language by other means. Another example from Whorf: Hopi requires a verb marking, called an *evidential*, like some other languages in the world also do. For example, is what you say based on what you saw for yourself or what you heard from other people?

These first levels of languaculture, starting from the basement—phonology (the sound system), morphology (word building), and syntax (sentence building)—are what most people think of when they think of "language" or "linguistics." The problem is that we're not done with the story yet. The next two levels involve semantics —what language means— and pragmatics—how language is used.

Still and all, you can find culture in those first three levels of languaculture, and those three levels are the foundation. It's not an accident that so many evolutionary researchers assert that the emergence of culture and the emergence of language occurred at the same time. *The same thing was emerging.* In contrast to the limited spaces of sound and grammar, the question of what language *means* and how to *use* it causes rashes to break out among traditional linguists.

A little history might be interesting here. In 1957 Noam Chomsky published a book called *Syntactic Structures*. Another name for his early theory is *generative grammar*. In his case, *generative* refers to the ability of a grammar to use a finite system of rules to produce an infinite number of sentences. But he also made several assumptions that isolated grammar from the rest of languaculture and abstracted it from the world of speakers and their contexts.

This was quite different from linguistic anthropology of the time. Linguistic anthropology was mostly aimed at fieldwork in the traditional descriptive way. It was about phonology, morphology, and syntax and how to figure them out in the language of the village you were working in, a language for which a published grammar was probably not available. In other words, it was training that made it possible to do fieldwork without an interpreter.

Chomsky changed linguistics, and kept changing it, in ways that go beyond the ability of this book to cover. The bottom line is that he moved away from the traditional anthropological use of linguistics as a prerequisite for the ethnographic study of culture. For him, language was a formal abstract system, something that was a biologically based human universal.

In response, anthropologists and sociologists and others created new kinds of linguistics to look at language as a means to the end of understanding some group of people. The social scientists wanted to build a scaffold to get to the more culturally loaded part of languaculture. The new Chomsky-style linguistics focused on phonology, morphology, and syntax and stayed there. Some of the next generation rebelled and tried to move in a semantic direction. Charles Fillmore, whose grammar was described earlier, is one example.

Among the new frameworks was something called *ethnographic semantics*, the field I trained in as a graduate student. Most of the early work focused on names for things, the idea being that small-*c* cultures dedicated a lot of the meaning in their language to things that were important to them for any number of reasons. Another new framework was called *sociolinguistics*. The idea here was that the use of language varied in a population—often variation in the less culturally loaded areas of phonology and syntax—the difference being that the variation was to be explained with social variables. If someone tells you to "Pahk the cah ovah theah," they're probably not from Texas. If someone calls a churchgoer a "penitent," it's probably not a wedding. These two approaches are only a sample of many early moves to counter Chomsky's new linguistics that separated language from speaker and hearer and context.

These and other approaches that flourished in reaction to Chomsky and continue to do so today zeroed in on parts of language that help with learning about a local "culture." Semantics—what words and sentences mean—gives a Chomsky-style linguist acid reflux. Hard not to react that way, with a paradigm that makes language abstract and biological and, as I heard Chomsky say in a lecture, a form of "mathematical neurophysiology." What do local meaning and ways of speaking have to do with it? Not a hell of a lot.

Words and sentences can mean anything, as long as people who use them agree. And if there isn't a word that means something, and the people who use the language want to express that meaning, they can make it so. Kids who learn the grammar of their native language do so starting around two years of age and progress with amazing speed. Learning how to communicate, to understand what others mean and to respond in some meaningful way in return— that process starts even earlier and continues to expand and change for the rest of one's life. For example, in the first year of life a human infant begins to do joint attention—that is, to follow the caregiver's gaze to the same thing in their shared world as the adult talks about it, the first lessons in what is *significant* in that world. And the famous play *My Fair Lady* is a sociolinguistic parable for adult learning in how to behave among the elites, as in tomaytos versus tomahtos.

It looks like there is more culture in semantics then there is in phonology or syntax, though without phonology and syntax there wouldn't be a system to organize the signifiers that carry those meanings. Making sense in a semantic kind of way is something animals are capable of, if they are trained by humans. As earlier observed, most can't speak because they don't have our vocal tract—though some birds come close—and their grammar doesn't get much more complicated than the two-year-old's "pivot grammar." (Pivot grammar is a stage in language acquisition consisting of a pivot word, like *allgone*, followed by an open slot. So you can get "allgone milk," "allgone cat," and so on.)

The signifier/signified connection is no longer an indivisible whole. Any signifier is made up of parts that can be combined and recombined in innumerable ways to mean different things. Every signified that can be experienced, remembered, or imagined can be paired with a unique signifier. How or why or how fast this languacultural ability happened is a matter of debate. Considering the traces left in the archaeological record, it probably happened fairly quickly in evolutionary terms. Fitch's argument, mentioned earlier, was that the pivotal event was the evolution of that wiring between the cortex and the vocal auditory system. Everything else for languaculture to take off, according to animal research and speculations about *Homo erectus*, was already there in simplified form.

In this scenario, the culture part of languaculture makes a stronger appearance with semantics than it did with sounds and grammar, but it owes its ability to do so to developments at those lower levels of languacultural organization. Once languaculture was unleashed, different groups built different worlds as they built arbitrary systems of signs to make sense out of what was significant in those worlds.

What kind of world do we live in? What kind of entities and events does it consist of? What sort of evaluations do we assign to them? Such questions—and their answers—could now be encoded in a system built on sounds.

We have one more level to go, the level I've been calling *communication*, a word that explicitly signals that something social is going on. One general name for that level is *pragmatics* (language in use). Phonology is about how languaculture sounds; morphology and syntax, about how it is structured; semantics, about what it means; pragmatics, about *how it is used*.

Pragmatics

Pragmatics, in the sense of language in use, is founded in part on what philosopher Paul Grice called "the cooperative principle," a nice preview of where we're going in the next chapter (1975). "Make your conversational contribution such as it is required, at the stage at which it occurs, by the accepted purpose or direction of the talk exchange in which you are engaged" (p. 45). This is how Grice summarized what users of languaculture expect when they communicate with each other. The expectation is for cooperation. If speakers do not follow the cooperative principle, then hearers will make inferences to figure out what the speaker meant by not cooperating. In other words, the basis of languaculture use is cooperation, even in cases of conflict.

Grice's principle arose, as far as I know, independently of the many other academic fields that ask why humans are more cooperative than other animals. Michael Tomasello's work shows how even a little kid in diapers will toddle over to see whether they can help an adult who is having a problem with an object (2011). One hypothesis might be that the benefits of languaculture while participating in a task with others in a band requires cooperation. In other words, cooperation emerged with languaculture to make it possible to improve task performance. More in the next chapter.

Another robust part of pragmatics is the concept of a *speech act*, first presented in a book with the title of *How to Do Things with Words* by John Austin (1975), another nice title that points at the next chapter. The core idea here is that certain actions are accomplished through language, sometimes involving the institutional authority of the speaker to perform that act by saying those words. One of his favorite examples is "I now pronounce you husband and wife." This simple sentence changes the relationship and requires a person authorized by society to sanction the change on its behalf. It creates the possibility of institutions.

Grice covered language and cooperation. Austin, in his book, covered language as a form of social action. Pragmatics is a huge field today, much more than I can cover here. The point for now is that the way that the Languaculture Big Bang linked to coordination in task performance shows up nicely in pragmatics. Like semantics, it is an area where the language/culture balance shifts toward the "cultural."

Pragmatics will come up frequently in this book. Pragmatics and semantics are the most cultural part of languaculture. Even if people use the same phonology, morphology, and syntax, the way that they *use* the language and what they *mean* by it is a minefield of languacultural differences. One of the early Western novels in the United States, *The Virginian*, is famous in part for just one line of dialogue: "When you call me that, smile." The cooperative principle has been violated by the villain, and the Virginian responds by firing a pragmatic warning shot across the bow, requesting that the villain show that he wasn't serious, while at the same time laying his pistol in plain sight on the card table in the Western saloon. That last part wasn't speech, but it certainly was an indexical semiotic act.

The focus in this book will be on languaculture in use. We're in good historical company here. Bronisław Malinowski argued that language use was where the heart of the meaning could be found. Ludwig Wittgenstein said that a form of language was a form of life. More recently, Daniel Everett (2012) argues that culture, cognition, and communication are the trifecta that explains language. These and other sources land where this book wants to land to answer a couple of questions. First, what was it about the world of *Homo sapiens* that made languaculture take off so quickly? Second, what is it about the world of contemporary *Homo sapiens* that guarantees languaculture will be a problem?

We'll see that the same mechanisms answer both questions, that what enabled new heights of cooperation in the ancestral hunter-gatherer world now guarantees conflict in the global society of the twenty-first century.

Raising a kid, hunting for food, building a dwelling, tending the garden, making music, telling the story of why the Moon waxes and wanes—local languaculture would make it easier to do all those things and figure out how to do them better. That ability to develop a group-specific semantics and pragmatics meant that each small hunting-gathering band would veer off onto its own languacultural path. With enough differences, sense making across groups would become difficult (if not impossible), and so would cooperation.

If two people with separate languacultures for a task are forced into that task and cooperation is necessary, those two people may have a problem.

If different phonologies and morphologies and syntaxes are involved, then interpreters and translators are required even to begin. If the people involved in the task, whether local or distant, know those three levels well enough to communicate, then semantics and pragmatics are the dangerous territory, especially for those who learned different languacultures for the task that circumstances now require them to jointly participate in.

The argument in this book is that global society makes these circumstances inevitable and frequent. Before we go there, though, let's look at what kind of world made this languaculture take off.

How Did Languaculture   **3**
Take Off So Fast?

NOW WE KNOW SOMETHING, or think we know something, about the Culture Big Bang. The *Languaculture* Big Bang, I should say now. We know something about how things came together to create new possibilities for the hominin line, and how those new possibilities allowed for different hunting-gathering bands to develop distinct local histories. But why did it take off so dramatically? The literature—not to mention common sense—argues that it made humans better at key tasks, like hunting, warfare, and child-rearing. No doubt true. Local languaculture would in principle improve the coordination for any task. And generativity increased the chances that someone would figure out a way to do the task better.

In order to understand the Languaculture Big Bang, though, we have to go beyond the world of biological evolution. Change no longer waits on the slow pace of natural selection. Now we fall into that difficult territory that mixes biology with all the fuzzy human stuff—mind, intentionality, society, history. Traditionally, in anthropology, a firm border was maintained between the two. Franz Boas, German immigrant and founder of academic American anthropology, wanted to keep biology out of culture—period. He was horrified by the eugenics movement in early twentieth-century America, not to mention what developed in his native country. On the other side of that boundary is the more recent book by biologist Richard Dawkins, *The Selfish Gene* (1976). According to him, your genes are going to do what they are going to do. You can make up whatever stories you like about who you think you are and what it is you think you're doing. In the end, it all boils down to heredity with variation and natural selection.

As soon as the word *evolution* comes up, *neo-Darwinism* is sure to follow. But after the Languaculture Big Bang, the long, slow dynamic of genetic transmission was no longer the only mechanism to promote evolutionary success. Now people could innovate and change a task to improve its outcome in real time, or even hinder it from a long-term evolutionary point of view.

Biological evolution is of course important. But once languaculture came into play all kinds of new possibilities for individual and social change could arise within a human lifetime—caused by human will and purpose, not genetic variability. And so, beginning in the 1960s, dual inheritance theory, or DIT—already mentioned in an earlier chapter—was born to include both (Boyd & Richerson, 1985). DIT required a look at the *coevolution* of genes and culture. For DIT the culture part is defined as "socially learned behavior."

As we have seen, many of the abilities that languaculture would support were present in simpler form among other animals and earlier forms of humanity. *Homo sapiens* had many more neocortical neurons available to wire and rewire. In particular, as mentioned earlier, the link between neocortex and vocal tract created the combinatorial explosion in signifiers that no longer required a direct connection with what was being signified. It enabled human speech to explode in its production of symbols.

So, how did all this speaking start? It certainly wasn't "de noche a mañana," as they say in Spanish—that is, "overnight." It probably happened rapidly (recall the acceleration of the S-curve) and diffused fairly quickly. Or maybe it happened according to the bottleneck theory. The speculation is that the Toba volcanic eruption reduced human population to between one thousand and ten thousand breeding pairs between fifty thousand and one hundred thousand years ago. The timing is right. And so are the conditions, the sudden onset of a severe volcanic winter that would have required rapid adaptation. Or maybe it was at the point when *Homo sapiens* first migrated out of Africa, the date of that event now being a point of contention, like everything else given the tremendous amount of work recently done on human evolution.

As I thought about this question—"How did it start?"—I also thought about Helen Keller. I wondered how she crossed over from her blind and deaf world into a world where communication was possible. Might she have exemplified the innovative edginess of some individual who suddenly figured out the infinite possibilities of the new vocal tract in an "aha" moment and then ran wild with it, along with the rest of the band? So I looked her up in *Wikipedia*. Here's what it said:

[Anne] Sullivan arrived at Keller's house in March 1887 and immediately began to teach Helen to communicate by spelling words into her hand, beginning with "d-o-l-l" for the doll that she had brought Keller as a present. Keller was frustrated, at first, because she did not understand that every object had a word uniquely identifying it. In fact, when Sullivan was trying to teach Keller the word for "mug," Keller became so frustrated she broke the mug. Keller's breakthrough in communication came the next month, when she realized that the motions her teacher was making on the palm of her hand, while running cool water over her other hand, symbolized the idea of "water"; she then nearly exhausted Sullivan demanding the names of all the other familiar objects in her world.

Those two bits of data—the bottleneck and the Keller epiphany—at least suggest the speculation. The Languaculture Big Bang may have occurred when the human population was small, struggling in a sudden and severe climate change caused by a volcanic eruption or by the migration out of Africa that urgently required some innovative adaptations. And the nature of the Languaculture Big Bang might have been more like an epiphany than learning a particular skill, because, once an individual "got it," it applied to virtually every task that one did and changed the way that one did them. If this speculation is anywhere near correct, you can see the need for constraints as well. A Helen Keller epiphany might have led to a naming orgy on the way to a hunter-gatherer Tower of Babel. Keller, according to *Wikipedia*, "nearly exhausted" her teacher once she realized she had entered new semiotic territory that featured duality of patterning—her sudden realization that an infinite number of signifiers were available to her.

However it happened, local languaculture grew in interaction with an environment. Now, with DIT, dual inheritance theory, *Homo sapiens* could change the way they did things themselves, in real time, depending on how other things were going. How did they rank tasks to decide which ones were the most important to modify first? And how did they decide whether the task was doing its job? It turns out that an age-old theory from the 1940s can help answer these questions: Maslow's hierarchy of needs (1943).

Languaculture Meets Needs

Imagine that the speculation about the Toba volcano, or migration into new lands, or just rude late Pleistocene weather, is right. An environmental change requires adaptation combined with the new ability to

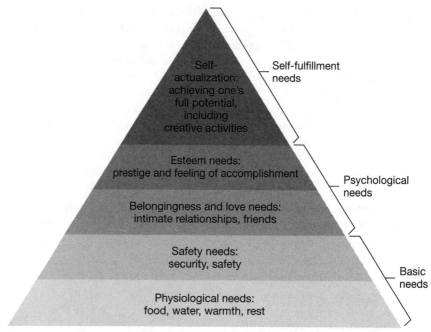

Figure 3.1. Maslow's Hierarchy of Needs

figure out different ways to adapt thanks to generativity. You need to change the way you do things—most things, in fact. The pressure is on to innovate, and fast.

There is a theory of human motivation that makes perfect sense here—namely, Maslow's hierarchy of needs. It is usually represented with a triangle, something like what is shown in figure 3.1.

In this chapter I'm going to emphasize the basic needs—physiological and safety. The four lower needs in the triangle—basic and psychological—are called *deficit needs*. That means that if they aren't being met, a person drops everything and takes care of them. And they are taken care of in reverse order of altitude, so physiological needs are first, then safety, and so on up the triangle. If you don't have food and water, you take care of that first. Once you're fed and watered, you worry about your security. If you are under threat, you take care of that before you worry about your intimate relationships and friends. And so on up the ladder to self-actualization, the optional fifth level, the contemporary epidemic disease of those who can afford the time for self-fulfillment.

As I think about the flow of events and channel my inner hunter-gatherer, it all seems plausible. A population of humans with as-yet-undeveloped languacultural abilities faces unexpected life-threatening surprises. Obviously they're not going to be concerned with the relative contributions of culture and biology and the interactions between the two. They're going to be concerned with figuring out how to eat and stay alive in a suddenly and surprisingly hostile environment.

Once someone in a particular band "got it," like in the Helen Keller epiphany, it's easy to imagine that the new duality-of-pattern trick would diffuse rapidly within that band. What I'm not sure about is the nature of social networks among the various hunting-gathering bands on the planet at the time of the volcanic eruption and/or the outmigration from Africa.

If it was a few thousand humans within a fairly limited geographical space, it is easy to imagine that the new ability would diffuse among different bands in no time at all. However, if the population was widely distributed, with minimal contact among bands, I don't know how to imagine the process of diffusion. Or perhaps it might be like Everett's account of bows and arrows (2012) and why you find them everywhere: since there are just so many ways of using naturally available materials to figure out how to hunt fast-moving animal protein, the inchoate languaculture (like the bow and arrow) might well have been an obvious ability to emerge and be put to work, across many different sites, particularly under a do-or-die environmental change. This issue—was it diffusion or independent invention—is an argument you'll find frequently in anthropology, history, and other social sciences and humanities.

Notice that I've avoided controversial arguments around group selection. I don't think it's a necessary concept to get the party started, and it would have worked too slowly to make the party possible at all, if the speculations here are at all in the ballpark. However, at the level of lived experience, those hunting-gathering bands that could innovate effectively in the face of dramatic change would live long and prosper while those who didn't would starve or lose out in conflict with other bands in the face of scarce resources. But, in the end, the Big Bang looks much more like an argument for quick change courtesy of languaculture rather than slow change in the gene pool.

Grooming with Words

So far, we have a small group of people confronted with a difficult environment. They would like to eat and stay alive. They have abilities in common with other animals and earlier humans for cognition and communication, though, unlike those other animals, they have more neurons and a direct connection to the vocal tract to control sound production. With that kind of environment, those kinds of ready-to-wear cognitive and communicative skills, as well as biological enhancements in brain and vocal tract, the rapid appearance of languaculture isn't so difficult to imagine.

Now tasks become more complicated, more variable, more effective in taking care of the deficit needs in Maslow's triangle. Many of them became more effective because they require coordination among several participants. In fact, this social coordination, argue some, is one reason why languaculture flourished. It's one possible answer to the question of why humans didn't sign like Deaf people do to communicate. The hypothesized answer is that speech left the hands free to do things.

But what did social networks look like? And what about biology in terms of inbreeding?

The size estimate for hunting-gathering bands varies. Let's say one hundred for the purpose of this thought experiment. Were they all related? No, probably several bands were in contact for marriage and trade. Or were they still all related in spite of exogamy, because the networks were still pretty small? With a small number of small bands in contact, how many marriage exchanges would it take until they all were part of the same gene pool? (Sounds like a problem from an arithmetic textbook.) Maybe it worked more like selective breeding of animals and plants to produce better strains? I'm still not clear on how inbreeding is both a bad and a good thing. Good for plants and animals, but bad for humans?

I have no idea how to answer these questions. It seems likely that for any hunting-gathering band, other bands in direct contact with them would all be related after a fairly short period of time. The incest taboo is a human universal, so it also seems likely that there was a prohibition against marriage between siblings early on. But there are societies where cousin marriage is preferred, like the small village where I worked in South India. In New Mexico, first-cousin marriage is not preferred, but it is allowed. Maybe it's an evolutionary trade-off—the chances of a harmful recessive allele decline enough with cousin distance and increase enough for advantageous allele pairs so that the sibling-incest taboo was sufficient as an evolutionarily stable strategy.

Task management now becomes a more complicated issue. In primate societies, the alpha male and female were in charge. That still worked no doubt in the hunting-gathering band, though "alpha-ness" becomes more complicated. It's not necessarily just who can beat up whom, though it can be that. But now there are lots of other ways to be recognized as an authority—skill at innovation, coordinating groups, communicating effectively and charismatically, task performance, and many other talents relevant to delivering results from tasks that keep the deficit needs at bay.

Task management implies rules of the game—in other words, local languaculture. What sort of general problems do these rules have to deal with? One general problem that exercises researchers of human cooperation and conflict nowadays is generally known as *collective-goods problems*—namely, what to do when there is a conflict between individual and group interests around some shared resource. How does a group keep its individual members in line?

Concepts familiar to the reader probably include the *tragedy of the commons*, where each person tries to get as much as they can from a common resource, thereby guaranteeing that that resource will be used up. Then there is the famous *prisoner's dilemma* game, structured so that the best choice for one player requires trust that the other player will act in the common good rather than only in his or her individual interest. There's the *free-rider* problem, where someone does not contribute to a group effort because they will benefit whether or not they pitch in. As usual, these questions are now applied to animal research as well (Nunn 2000, for example). Animals have collective-goods problems, too.

In a small group like the hunter-gatherer band right after the Languaculture Big Bang, where everyone probably has a consanguineal or affinal relationship to everyone else, and where the band regularly faces severe disruption in their physiological and safety needs, it looks like any free rider would be rapidly noticed and just as rapidly brought into line. Same deal with the tragedy of the commons: the greedy would be noticed skulking in the night. And research with the prisoner's dilemma game shows that—surprise, surprise—if players play repeatedly and are allowed to communicate, they figure out how to make the best possible collective choice based on reputation earned in previous play. Such contemporary theoretical problems would be quickly observed and resolved among band members in the ancestral condition.

I know that there are many languaculture universals related to managing collective-goods issues, and I know it's a good guess that they were part of the Languaculture Big Bang. At this point, I don't want to shift into a book that represents a post–Big Bang languacultural theory of how hunter-gatherer bands work. But I would like to offer at least one example related to the collective-action problem. Are there some features of languaculture that might have addressed such management problems in the ancestral condition?

Consider the topic of gossip. My computer dictionary defines gossip as "casual or unconstrained conversation or reports about other people, typically involving details that are not confirmed as being true." I'm not sure about the "not confirmed" part. In most gossiping I've heard or done, the gossiper swears on their mother's grave that what they are about to report is true and newsworthy. The fact that the truth can get seriously distorted in service of making the content newsworthy (and, in my experience, often is) seldom damages the willing suspension of disbelief among the audience. As one news reporter said, "If it bleeds, it leads."

There is a substantial literature on gossip. It is a major point of intersection for pragmatics and culture. Well, it is now. In the 1980s, the topic of gossip was looked down upon by the academically entrenched. But in 1987 I was visiting a communications group in Sweden. So was Jörg Bergmann, who had just published his book on gossip, called *Klatsch*, that same year. Some readers will know of Deborah Tannen's work on the different pragmatics of speaking among men and women (1990), which includes some comments on gossip. Later Robin Dunbar wondered whether language developed to substitute gossip for grooming among primates as a way for humans to keep track of social relationships (1996).

If you're a soap opera fan, gossip is also a genre of language where—if you can get phonology, syntax, and semantics in order (and often even if you can't)—you will find some universally recognizable content. For many scenes, you won't need language at all. Things like facial expression and body language and tone of voice will convey betrayal and hypocrisy, as well as praise, both faint and extravagant. Gossip is one way to learn what you need to know to evaluate the trustworthiness and reputation of others. It is a universal languaculture genre.

Hunting-gathering bands are said to have been egalitarian in their social organization. Certainly there would be personality differences, leaders, recognition of experts in some tasks, and conflicts at times among band members. But in a harsh environment, with the lower levels of Maslow's pyramid frequently calling out for attention, and with the biological changes that enabled phonology, it's not hard to imagine languaculture and task taking off together in an amplifying feedback loop.

We could continue the speculation using more areas of languaculture, especially from semantics and pragmatics. And it might not have had to diffuse at a bottleneck moment, after the volcanic explosion or when early *Homo sapiens* first left Africa. It's not hard to imagine that Helen Keller–type epiphanies would occur independently among many different bands once the critical missing piece of biological infrastructure was in place. Nor is it hard to imagine that languaculture and the tasks of hunter-gatherer life would leave a trail of new practices and constraints that quickly developed a variety of different local languacultures.

Contemporary collective-action researchers argue over what explains human cooperation. I don't think it's that complicated to understand from the point of view of the lived experience of hunter-gatherers in the ancestral condition. Languaculture enabled more innovation and cooperation, Maslow's needs demanded it, the environment made it a priority, and better task performance and population growth rewarded it. Cooperation emerged as a result of the interaction of languaculture and task and environment.

This works—at least it's plausible—for small groups of hunter-gatherers fifty thousand years ago. And it was the situation for the next forty thousand or so years of modern *Homo sapiens*. Things began to change with the appearance of settled agriculture. And now, as recently announced in the journal *Science* (Wigginton, 2016), the same modern *Homo sapiens* have pushed Earth into a new geological epoch, starring themselves, called the Anthropocene. Those changes, so goes the premise of this book, have turned languaculture into a frequent and recurring problem. So let's take a panoramic view of one possible way to understand how to handle them better.

Why Did It Stop Working?   4

GENERATIVITY AND CONSTRAINTS—the perfect evolutionary match. Balanced properly, with an occasional lurch in one direction or the other, they hum along in the background of life in a hunting-gathering band and keep them innovative enough to come up with bright ideas but stable enough to take care of adaptive business. Just the right mix of disorder and order, the mix that complexity science says is part and parcel of any living system moving through time.

There's a problem with this happy ending, though. These generative and constraint mechanisms evolved to work in a world that no longer exists. In the ancestral condition, they stored the incremental results of local history by creating a *tradition*, a sanctioned way of doing things, a social flywheel that weighed on individual action. Experiments from social psychology show some of those constraint mechanisms in living color. In those experiments, humans look like conservative creatures, following the demands of peers and authority, spiteful toward outsiders and their different ways, and arrogant in their belief that only they see the world as it really is.

In our brave new global world, this won't do. "Global" is, of course, not news. In that vast time period between fifty thousand years ago and now, large-scale societies rose and fell, many of them, like today, driven by trade or religion or some mix of the two. For millennia humans have lived in places shaped by the influence of distant lands. In 1937, the anthropologist Ralph Linton made fun of Americans' denial of this simple fact, producing along the way what has become a staple of introductory anthropology courses. In retrospect, the denial was insane at that time, given the global economic depression and the brewing world war. Linton called his article "One Hundred Percent American." It appeared in the *American Mercury* magazine. Here are some excerpts from the article (you can also find copies of different versions all over the web).

> There can be no question about the average American's Americanism or his desire to preserve this precious heritage at all costs. Nevertheless, some insidious foreign ideas have already wormed their way into his civilization without his realizing what was going on. Thus dawn finds the unsuspecting patriot garbed in pajamas, a garment of East Indian origin; and lying in a bed built on a pattern which originated in either Persia or Asia Minor. He is muffled to the ears in un-American materials: cotton, first domesticated in India; linen, domesticated in the Near East; wool from an animal native to Asia Minor; or silk whose uses were first discovered by the Chinese. . . .
>
> On awakening he glances at the clock, a medieval European invention; uses one potent Latin word in abbreviated form, rises in haste, and goes to the bathroom. Here, if he stops to think about it, he must feel himself in the presence of a great American institution; he will have heard stories of both the quality and frequency of foreign plumbing and will know that in no other country does the average man perform his ablutions in the midst of such splendor. But the insidious foreign influence pursues him even here. Glass was invented by the ancient Egyptians, the use of glazed tiles for floors and walls in the Near East, porcelain in China, and the art of enameling on metal by Mediterranean artisans of the Bronze Age. Even his bathtub and toilet are but slightly modified copies of Roman originals. The only purely American contribution to the ensemble is the steam radiator, against which our patriot very briefly and unintentionally places his posterior. . . .
>
> Returning to the bedroom, the unconscious victim of un-American practices removes his clothes from a chair, invented in the Near East, and proceeds to dress. He puts on close-fitting tailored garments whose form derives from the skin clothing of the ancient nomads of the Asiatic steppes and fastens them with buttons whose prototypes appeared in Europe at the Close of the Stone Age. . . . He puts on his feet stiff coverings made from hide prepared by a process invented in ancient Egypt and cut to a pattern which can be traced back to ancient Greece, and makes sure they are properly polished, also a Greek idea. Lastly, he ties about his neck a strip of bright-colored cloth which is a vestigial survival of the shoulder shawls worn by seventeenth century Croats. He gives himself a final appraisal in the mirror, an old Mediterranean invention, and goes downstairs to breakfast.

Here a whole new series of foreign things confronts him. His food and drink are placed before him in pottery vessels, the popular name of which—china—is sufficient evidence of their origin. His fork is a medieval Italian invention and his spoon a copy of a Roman original. He will usually begin his meal with coffee, an Abyssinian plant first discovered by Arabs. The American is quite likely to need it to dispel the morning-after effects of overindulgence in fermented drinks, invented in the Near East; or distilled ones, invented by the alchemists of medieval Europe. . . .

If our patriot is old-fashioned enough to adhere to the so-called American breakfast, his coffee will be accompanied by an orange, domesticated in the Mediterranean region, a cantaloupe domesticated in Persia, or grapes domesticated in Asia Minor. . . . From this he will go on to waffles, a Scandinavian invention, with plenty of butter, originally a Near-Eastern cosmetic. . . .

Breakfast over . . . [h]e then sprints for his train—the train, not the sprinting, being an English invention. At the station, he pauses for a moment to buy a newspaper, paying for it with coins invented in ancient Lydia. Once on board he settles back to inhale the fumes of a cigarette invented in Mexico, or a cigar invented in Brazil. Meanwhile, he reads the news of the day, imprinted in characters invented by the ancient Semites by a process invented in Germany upon a material invented in China. As he scans the latest editorial pointing out the dire results to our institutions of accepting foreign ideas, he will not fail to thank a Hebrew God in an Indo-European language that he is one hundred percent (decimal system invented by the Greeks) American (from Americus Vespucci, Italian geographer).

Regional—if not global—influence started long before Linton wrote his satire. Somewhere around twelve thousand years ago, agriculture emerged, leading to settled communities based on domesticated crops and animals. About six thousand years ago, city-states appeared, with division of labor turning more complicated and clear social strata appearing. Then empires developed, perhaps four thousand years ago, empires based on central control of large socially diverse areas. Greece and Rome are the examples usually emphasized in European and American education, but empires started before they did and happened in many other parts of the world.

With so many regional moments since the Languaculture Big Bang, why claim that something unique is going on with globalization now? Isn't this just another example of the long human story of social evolution? Another S-curve moment, if you remember that curve from chapter 1? A sudden transition followed by a new period of stability? On the face of it, that curve isn't a bad model for the shift to agriculture, to city-state, and then to nation-state. A critical point is reached, then a comparatively rapid transition from one social form to another occurs—rapid being relative to the pace of what preceded and followed the change—and then the curve flattens out again.

Our current global tangle is that—another growth spurt—but it's also something more. Consider figure 4.1's graph of technology innovation over roughly the previous century. It takes a moment to get used to the format. The x-axis, the horizontal scale, starts with the baseline year when a technology was invented (*year 1*). The new technologies obviously were not all invented at the same time, but they all had a year 1. So the lines all start at the same place.

Each line represents a different technology. The y-axis, the vertical scale, is the percentage of people who used the new technology as of 1997, the time the graph was originally published in *Forbes*. It goes without saying that the internet, PC, and cell phone lines have skyrocketed in the past twenty years. The curves show how rapidly a particular technology is adopted and how the older curves finally flatten out.

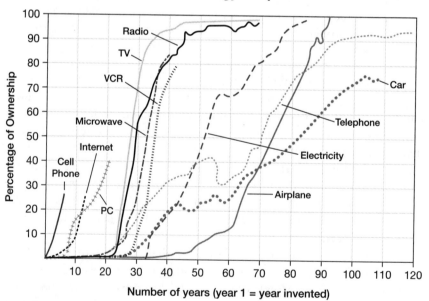

Figure 4.1.
Source: Adapted from *Forbes*

Two things are striking about this picture. One is that the family of curves has more or less the same logistic growth shape used to describe rapid change elsewhere in the book, including the Big Bang. This makes intuitive sense, because many of the technologies in the graph are part of the litany of explanations of how we suddenly became a global society—transportation and communication and media are featured. Globalization and those technologies coevolved with amplifying feedback loops. Nothing new there.

But the second striking thing is more important. The technologies in the graph are almost all *social-network extenders*, and there are a lot of them. Electricity is more general than that, but, still, most items in the graph represent technologies that make social connections possible, more quickly and easily, some of them connections that simply couldn't have been made a century earlier without massive time and effort. And the connections, by and large, make it possible to forge direct links to large numbers of distant people.

Previous technological change in the human story was more about production of goods. The important *social* networks remained local, face-to-face. The royal houses traded spouses far and wide, and the occasional explorer or trader wandered off for years and returned with exotic tales and new products—what would Italy be without the tomatoes that the Spanish conquistadores brought back from Mexico?—but for most of the fifty thousand years of modern human history, people lived in a social world only within reach of foot—or hoof—and mouth.

The graph shows a dramatic change in *technologies for social connection*. Technology doesn't just diffuse through a network now; technology *extends* the network itself even as it diffuses. Technology diffusion is *self-referential—if you adopt the technology from your social network, then your own network extends*—and when things get self-referential, all hell breaks loose. Just ask Kurt Gödel.

This technology makes for a flat Earth, as Thomas Friedman called it in his recent book (2005). Time and distance don't matter as much anymore. Any person can, in principle, quickly and easily connect to any other person. And the connection isn't limited to one person but extends to several of them, all at once, as well as to the knowledge that they produce and the institutions in which they participate.

Some of the changes are about transportation. Bodies move more easily and over greater distances, all the time—migration, refugees, an international workforce, exchange programs, war, and the list goes on. Even if a body doesn't move, other bodies move to it, through all of the above means plus through images, film and cable broadcasts, internet connections, products, disease, translations, and so on. Global technologies snapped global society into focus recently enough so it still surprises many of us today who lived the transition as it really took off. My high-tech colleagues—a generation younger than me—refer to *their* younger generation as "digital natives." They don't hunt and gather until after they log on.

How did this global social network come about? Obviously, hunter-gatherer bands were a network. Obviously, modern humans form a network as well. And—the final obviously—the two networks are very different from each other. The point of this obviousness is that those differences will help explain how languaculture changed from an adaptive advantage to a dysfunctional problem.

From culture with a Small *c* to Hybrid

How do we compare these before and after networks to better see the differences? I don't want to make this book an introduction to social-network theory, but I'd like to use a couple of its concepts to clarify how that graph of technology adoptions made the world a different place. Network theory is another S-curve growth kind of area that would require a second book to review. It starts by connecting entities with lines to make a picture of what is connected with what. Think of a subway map or a picture of the electric grid. *Social* networks connect up people or their organizations instead of underground stations or power plants.

Imagine we started with a question: "Who do you drink coffee with at least once a month?" We draw lines connecting you with those people. Then we ask the people you mentioned who *they* drink coffee with and add them to the diagram. Then we ask the people that those people mentioned who they drink coffee with. We are now two steps away from you, and the picture of the local coffee-drinking world begins to emerge. Clusters start to form when people who drink coffee with people you named also say they drink coffee with you.

How far out does this madness go? I drink coffee with a Swedish colleague on Skype. Since my colleague is eight hours later on the clock, she might drink wine. Do I drink coffee with her or not?

Social-network studies usually draw boundaries around some population and focus on only one, or at most a few, specific kinds of connection. So, for example, "Who are your best friends?" (asked of students at a particular high school). Or "Who do you have lunch with at least once a week?" (asked of members of a particular organization). High school re-

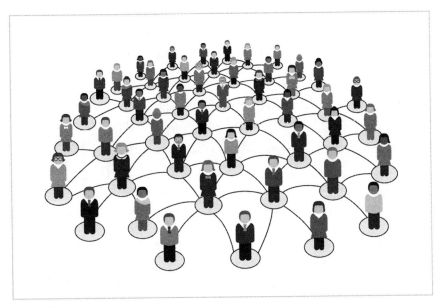

Figure 4.2.
Source: iStock Essentials/aelitta

search usually produces a picture that dramatically displays a racial divide. Organizational research usually shows that the lunch groups have a way of running rings around the formal organizational chart.

Now we need a few pieces of network jargon. Figure 4.2 is a picture of a network, much too neat for government work, but something to get us started. This network is what is called a "giant component." That just means there is a path from anyone in the network to anyone else, whether directly or through intermediaries. The graph doesn't have to be so neat, and it seldom is. In real research there are usually some disconnected outliers, either individuals or small groups of them. Remember high school?

Stuart Kauffman set up a computer experiment to show how a giant component can form in an S-curve sort of way (1995). Picture an empty space on the computer screen. Now create a bunch of critters, and toss them into that empty space. The program picks two critters that are not connected to each other, at random, and draws a line between them. Then it picks two more critters that aren't connected, again at random, and connects them. It keeps doing this.

The weird thing is this: When the average number of connections is about one per critter, as if by magic, a *giant component* emerges. Recall that a giant component means that, all of a sudden, in a logistic growth kind of way, all the critters are connected with each other, either directly or with a few hops from one critter to another. Separate clusters of critters appear and grow as the program runs. Suddenly there is a completely connected network.

It really is fascinating to watch. If you're curious, see "NetLogo Example 2: Giant Component," at https://www.youtube.com/watch?v=Rl0gotu DcJg. Giant components will keep happening, over and over, all of a sudden, right around when the graph shows an average of one connection per critter.

But now we're not just dealing with a specific school or a specific organization. Now we are dealing with *all the humans on the planet*. So here's the argument based on the jargon: The network-extending technology displayed in the earlier graph shortened possible connections among everyone and made massive new connections available by direct search without intermediaries. At least that's the hypothesis here. A *global* giant component is something new, a configuration of the earthly human social world that never existed before.

The old way of thinking—that a social network means a connection with an actual person in the same physical location—that isn't the only way it works now. In my self-employed world, I have a large virtual network, but I have little to do with neighbors who live on either side of me or with people who live in the same town. Most of my face-to-face contacts are in the coffee shop where I like to work and the gym where I like to work out, and both those places have Wi-Fi so I can check email and look up things that I've been wondering about all day. There is one guy who sometimes appears in both places, like I do, so there's a potential first step toward a local link. But he refuses to talk with anybody.

Local face-to-face small groups—the mainstay of the hunting-gathering band, and for that matter most of human history—they play less of a role in how the world works now. But those groups were *the* original source of languaculture based on shared tasks done together, and that languaculture was designed to keep those face-to-face groups coherent and consistent. There is clearly something wrong with this picture when we apply that traditional notion of "culture" to the social world that technology hath wrought today.

Linton, in his essay about the 100 percent American, made it sound like global worlds have been around for millennia. True in terms of historical connections and diffusion of objects. But the argument here is that a major change occurred, a tipping point into a global giant component, made possible by technology that "compresses time and space," as Steger summarizes globalization (2003). With all the network extenders, we can pretty much find anyone we want from the privacy of our coffee shop.

Anthropologists have noticed. In a personal communication, Russ Bernard made the same point: "This means that today, there are no longer any cultures—only ethnic groups. That is, there are cultures embedded in a multicultural political unit called, for the moment, the state. In the near future, we can imagine superstates to emerge and to be called something else. The methods for studying cultures embedded in multicultural political units are just now coming to light." It's not that "cultures" are embedded in states—or not only that. Nation-states also have fuzzy boundaries. In fact, fuzzy is the name of the game. Recall the discussion of hybrids—much more to come. The network-extending technologies and the planet-wide giant component that they make possible help us understand that hybrids are probably the new normal. Specifically, the planet-wide flow of social influences—local to global and everything in between—results in a breed of human that defies simple categorization in terms of a single "culture."

Global giant components have created hybrids who need to cooperate in tasks that they may well have different views of. Then again, it's hard to predict with hybrids. They might have the *same* task perspective even though, from the outside looking in, major "cultural" differences were expected. Or they might have wildly different task perspectives even though an outsider expected "cultural" similarity. Hybrids don't just blur "cultural" or "national" lines; they blur them all, both within the hybrid him- or herself and between hybrids.

A little additional jargon shows how it's even more complicated than that. Earlier we built a hypothetical network based on the question of who drinks coffee with whom. That's probably a fairly pleasant kind of task. (Remember, *task* in this book just means at least two people doing something together.) But the coffee question shows how any task can generate a network—as in "With whom do you do task X?" In other words, every task is a potential "network-generating predicate," just like "Who do you drink coffee with?"

Now, consider the list of all the tasks that a hunter-gatherer would describe as part of their everyday life. If you ask people in one hunter-gatherer band with whom they do each task on the list, you're going to get a lot of overlap in the answers. In other words, the people you hunt and gather with, or eat with, or play games with, or share childcare with, or build a shelter with, or just hang around and shoot the breeze with—a lot of the same people will appear in many task networks.

Such networks are called *multiplex*, like the movie theaters. It means that for any pair of people in the network there are going to be a lot of different task-based links connecting them. For example, a family network—probably coextensive with band membership and marriage and trade links to other nearby bands—shows up over and over again in other tasks that you do.

Now readers can do a similar exercise for their own life. Assuming you're an employee in some metropolitan area, you are probably involved in several different non-overlapping networks. Participating in them will involve many of the social-network extenders from the previous technology adoption graph. Although you are now part of the global giant component, the networks for all the tasks in your life overlap much less. Many of the links will be single—that is, *uniplex*. In fact, it can be a little disorienting when a uniplex link from one task network shows up in the context of another task. The other day a colleague from the water field showed up in the gym. It took a while to figure out how to talk with each other, until we realized that you can talk about water in a gym even though you're sweaty and wearing shorts.

We've gone in a mere fifty thousand years from a small social world of relatively stable multiplex networks to a large dynamic global world of uniplex networks made up of hybrids. It's not quite that clean a generalization, but there's truth in the tendency. Now the actions of people that you didn't even know you were connected to, people far away, can land in a task at your doorstep in a surprising way.

Often it's a pleasant surprise, like a new Facebook friend who actually does become one, or an ability to shop on your computer during a boring meeting, or checking Twitter for the latest fake news. Terrorism is an obvious contemporary bad example, a "task" that you didn't choose to participate in, that drops you down into basic needs in Maslow's hierarchy, where you have no immediate network to help out, and where you have trouble finding the right connection to get information and help.

Social-network theory contains many more concepts and applications, the more so when it gets translated into its mathematical foundations in graph theory. The point for this section has been made. Think back to that technology adoption graph. Starting in the late nineteenth century, and accelerating since, new social-network-extending technologies have diffused and created a global giant component for the first time in human history. The results are particularly striking when we compare them to the small, stable multiplex networks of the ancestral condition.

Networks now link anyone on Earth with everyone else on Earth, on the fly, at a moment's notice—at least in principle—often in task-specific relationships that don't carry over into other tasks. Life is more uniplex and globally extended now. The flow through this global giant component makes it an odds-on bet that most on the planet are hybrids. Not everyone, but the younger you go, the more likely it is. The social forces that shape and change you are "downloaded" from the rest of the world, not just from your own face-to-face world.

Since languaculture developed in part as a constraint to dampen the new innovative abilities after the Languaculture Big Bang, we have a problem here. We're no longer dealing with a clearly bounded small group where you coordinate most tasks you do with the same people over and over again. Now we're dealing with two people who may never have met before, who have been shaped by many different social networks—some of them the same, some different—both in their own biography and by comparison with each other.

It's not clear what kind of languacultural situation we're going to have here. It is clear that two people will often be following different kinds of constraints that hinder the ability to innovate that we all acquired in the Languaculture Big Bang.

In the serious game I described earlier, the one designed to train Americans for Afghan "culture," we used things like conversational openings and indirect speech to teach Americans how to have a conversation with Afghans. The model for the Afghan game avatar was an elderly rural peasant, probably Pashtun in the minds of those knowledgeable enough to know there are four major distinct "cultural" groups in that country.

I used to like to tease my colleagues with this question: What if the American graduate of our game started into the elaborate three-part conversational opening we had trained him or her to do, and the Afghan said in perfect English, "Cut to the chase, dude," because he got his bachelor's degree in business at UCLA and knows more about the hypothetical contract-signing exercise than the American does?

As time goes on, the human world gets closer and closer to hybrids all the way down. And hybrids mean that no "cultural" template based on the ancestral condition can be confidently relied upon to describe or explain the problem when the hybrids hit a task glitch and try to figure out how to fix it.

Small Worlds Are Smaller than Global Giant Components

This global giant component is probably the second major social-network tipping point that ever happened. Duncan Watts, author of one of the better social network introductions, describes the appearance of the *small-world* network (2003). Readers might have seen the 1993 film *Six Degrees of Separation*, premised on that concept. Those familiar with small worlds might wonder, "Doesn't that mean that we already had a global giant component?" No, not really.

A small-world network means this: A person is part of social networks that are most of their local social world, the ancestral hunting-gathering band being a perfect example. But that network, if it is of the small-world variety, will always have a person or two in it who is connected to someone in a different network. It turns out that you can take a world of many separate networks—think hunting-gathering bands again—and just by adding a few far-flung connections among them, you magically get the famous six degrees of separation. That means, on average, you are just six hops away from everyone else in the entire world. People in those networks *do not know how connected they are*. They probably just know about that first hop, from someone in their group to someone who is a link to another group.

The difference now, to preview where this section is headed, is that the global component makes it easier to connect directly with far-flung networks, without any unknown intermediaries. With the global social world one meets them online or finds their web page and looks them up on the internet and emails them or gives them a call on Skype.

In Buenos Aires a while back I was browsing in a bookstore and found a book on complexity theory by an anthropologist, Carlos Reynoso. At the time it was rare to find this mixture anywhere (and still is). I went to the coffee shop with my laptop, found his email address, and sent one off and that night had dinner at his house. No connecting link necessary. Well, there was the book, obviously, but then the Gutenberg press was one of the first social network extenders.

Small worlds weren't there at the beginning, though, as Watts shows with an example: Imagine a map of the spread of the bubonic plague in fourteenth-century Europe. If Europe had been a small world then, the plague would have jumped from one place to another place quite distant, like diseases do now. It did that somewhat, via ships arriving in a port, but by and large that's not what happened. What happened was that the plague spread—for the most part—like a slowly moving wave, bit by bit across the European landscape. Social networks in a particular place only connected with other social networks near them. The plague moved along adjacent networks in direct contact with each other. Judging by this example, small worlds were an intermediate step between local hunting-gathering bands and global social networks.

Stanley Milgram first demonstrated the small world in social psychology in the 1960s (1967). However, the experiments themselves, as it turns out, were pretty flawed. For example, the researchers would give a card to someone in the Midwest and tell that person the name of a target in Boston. The subject was supposed to send the card on to someone who had a better chance of knowing someone who knew the target. The main problem was that most people wouldn't play. The intermediate links would often just quit.

But in one study, sixty-four letters did in fact reach their targets, about 30 percent of those that started out. The average number of hops it took to reach the target person in Boston was, in fact, that magical number six. Hence the saying: we're all connected to everyone in the world by *six degrees of separation.*

So sometime between the plague in the fourteenth century and the Milgram study in the 1960s, the planet went from isolated networks to networks connected—whether people in those networks knew it or not (and you can tell by Milgram's work that they didn't)—to every other person on Earth. But now, so goes the argument of this book, we've gone beyond small worlds into a global giant component. Now we live in an even more socially connected world. Now global connections mean that the world isn't just small—it's *compressed.* We don't need intermediaries to access an unknown distant part of the network anymore; we can directly connect.

The global network is replacing the old face-to-face network of most of *Homo sapiens'* history. After the small world appeared, local social networks still played the dominant role in a person's life. But now I think the face-to-face local network is fading in importance. If that network is fading, what's left? The far-flung ties. We've gone from (mostly) local clusters to small worlds (local clusters with a few far-flung ties) to (mostly) far-flung ties.

The change from local cluster to global giant component makes that local cluster less relevant to the way we live now. If that is correct, then the constraint mechanisms of languaculture really are dinosaurs. They evolved to *preserve* and *bound* the small face-to-face social network of a hunting-gathering band. The global world erodes their significance but continues with the constraint mechanisms designed to hold them in place. The constraint mechanisms that adapted the ancestral condition to the Languaculture Big Bang are maladaptive now.

The Hybrids 5

L ET'S TALK ABOUT HYBRIDS. Because of technological innovation and the emergence of global society, odds are that our pair of humans engaged in a task will both be hybrids.

This is an interesting mess I've dragged us into. Neither of our two humans will correspond to any simple languacultural template, but they want to have a languaculture in common that lets them accomplish a particular task.

This makes life more difficult than in the old days. Back then, it was about inter-*cultural* encounters. Now it is about inter-*hybrid* encounters. And hybrids are a mix and match—maybe mismatch—of many different kinds of social influences, some local, some global, some from somewhere in between. This means that instead of learning a template and applying it to a person who is a member of the category that the template supposedly labels, you have to figure out the person for yourself. You can no longer assume that any label will be a simple match that predicts what you should do or how the other person will react.

Here's a couple of stories to make the point. Japan and Malaysia are two places about which an American can find lots of books and workshops and web pages that give advice on how to handle those two "cultures."

I was heading home from a conference in Kobe. A publisher was translating my book *The Professional Stranger* into Japanese. He asked me to stop off in Tokyo and spend an evening getting to know each other.

We were to meet at five in the afternoon. I took the elevator down to the hotel lobby. It played soft background sounds of birds chirping. I was dressed informally, something like tan Levis and a short-sleeved shirt. The main Japanese phrase I had learned was "Hot, isn't it?" I got off the elevator, and Muryama looked informal as well, something like an alligator shirt and a casual sport coat. We walked toward each other. He slipped his hand into his side coat pocket.

Damn, I thought, *the business card!* Any of the popular stuff you read, any intercultural communication workshop you take, will make a big deal out of the presentation of business cards in Japan. With two hands even. Or at least they did then. I knew that as well as anyone who paid attention to "culture." But then his hand froze in the pocket. We kept approaching each other from across the lobby. He resumed his smile, pulled his empty hand out of his coat pocket, and we shook.

Muryama had visited the United States, was about my age, and had obviously decided "the hell with business cards, this guy isn't the type." I wasn't in Kansas anymore, but I wasn't in the Japan of the "Japanese culture" literature, either. One of our main topics of conversation at dinner was the 1960s and 1970s at Berkeley and Tokyo universities. Another was the international "pachinko" game of publishing. Thanks to a shared global history and mutual participation in a global industry, we were both hybrids with plenty of overlap.

A few years later I was talking about qualitative methods at a meeting of Southeast Asian epidemiologists in Penang, in Malaysia. One of the group was an Islamic Malaysian woman, conservatively dressed, always in a headscarf, who—as she later told me—agreed with the Malaysian politician Anwar's argument that Islam and contemporary global life were perfectly compatible. During the conference she was outspoken, critical, irreverent, direct, and (in my opinion) one of the smartest and most interesting people there. She would've made Gloria Steinem proud.

We were talking during a coffee break. She had recommended a book to me, an essay by a Malay journalist who had returned to the country and written about it. I told her that the book broke down all the stereotypes I'd read and heard about when it came to "Malaysian culture." Yes, she said, visitors come to the country, and then they get confused "when they meet somebody like me."

Muryama did think about a business card. (I later learned that Japanese syntax requires you to know something about relative social positions of speaker and hearer and person spoken about. A business card exchange helps with orientation before you have to talk. And notice, if you haven't already, that this is one of those moments when "culture" pokes its nose directly into syntax.) My Malaysian colleague did wear conservative Islamic Malay dress. And both she and Muryama were speaking English, a second language for each of them. Fluency—real fluency, close to native-speaker competence—in a second language learned as an adult pretty much guarantees hybridity. It means that one has added major different social influences to one's hybrid repertoire.

My Mental Model of Your Perspective

Remember earlier how Donald used the concept of *mental model* in his description of mimetic culture, with the example of the ham sandwich sitting at table 5? Let's continue to use the term here, but now we need to refine the meaning. Mental model no longer will refer to something another person "has." Instead, it will only refer to something a person—like you or me—puts together to make sense out of another person, from the outside looking in. It is *our* model of *them*, not *their* model. The word we will use for what that other person "has," for the way they see things, will be *perspective*. More about these two concepts in the next section.

Using these concepts we can summarize. The problem with this languaculture business is as follows:

1. Perspectives within an imposed "cultural" category can vary all over the place.
2. Perspectives from different sources mix and (mis)match, for different people in different ways.
3. The same person's mix can vary from one task to another and change over time.
4. Even a strong probability that "cultural" category X implies perspective characteristic Y won't necessarily predict a particular individual doing a specific task. Ask your local statistics maven. It's called the *ecological fallacy*.

Here's the *Wikipedia* definition: "An ecological fallacy (or ecological inference fallacy) is a formal fallacy in the interpretation of statistical data where inferences about the nature of individuals are deduced from inference for the group to which those individuals belong." The argument in this book is that the fallacy increases with hybridity, and hybridity is riding a logistic growth curve today.

It's Always the Universal in the Particular

In earlier chapters of this book, I had to drag the reader through culture and language in both capital and lowercase versions. It was necessary because that is the starting point for most people when they engage these concepts. With "languaculture" we got rid of the culture-language distinction. Now we need to get rid of the upper–lowercase split.

The reader has already noticed the slippery slope between the two. Generativity, the human universal, produced innovations that in turn became local constraints for the band that in turn limited future innovations. Or, with language, case grammar offered a flexible universal model that could fit a variety of specific, local, task-based communication needs. The moral of the story is that the universal-local distinction distorts as much as the one that separates language and culture. As Robert Redfield put it, good human science, like good literature, is "a glimpse of the eternal in the light of the ephemeral" (1948, p. 185). Universal and local are both part of any mental model that an outsider might build of another person's perspective.

Donald Brown lit a fire under the search for universals (1991). Like most senior anthropologists, he had been trained to focus on local differences. A brief summary of his epiphany in a bizarre high-tech setting can be viewed at https://www.youtube.com/watch?v=HNJSQAL0sEo, which shows his Pangea Day presentation. He opens with a story from his fieldwork in Brunei. A young man insisted on sitting at a lower level than him, an offense to Brown's egalitarian values. The young man explained that he was showing respect. "Showing respect" was a human universal, Brown realized, though signified in a different way. I agree with his conclusion that human universals are *the* great neglected territory for a powerful and useful theory of what it means to be human.

Laura Bohannon wrote one of my favorite stories, "Shakespeare in the Bush," back in 1966 to show human universals dancing with variable constraints. You can read it at http://www.naturalhistorymag.com/edi tors_pick/1966_08-09_pick.html. Highly recommended.

Bohannon told the story of Hamlet to the Tiv, a Nigerian tribe she was working with. Her audience corrected what they saw as obvious errors. For example, they had no trouble with the idea of a chief, but they knew that it was impossible for a dead chief to walk around. It had to be an omen sent by a witch instead. When the chief's brother married his wife after he was killed, that made perfect sense to the listeners. That he did it quickly was praiseworthy, not suspicious. That the chief had a wife went without saying; that he had only one made no sense. And on and on it goes, page after delightful page in Bohannon's funny and self-deprecating style.

For the Tiv, some parts of Hamlet made perfect sense right away, because those parts shared a universal human reality with Bohannon the storyteller and Shakespeare the author. But other parts of Hamlet were obvious errors, according to Tiv naïve realism, because they didn't fit local perspectives for how those universals worked in their social world.

Several times in this book, I have foreshadowed the argument that the way around problems in an inter-hybrid encounter is to move up in scale from local specifics to human universals where common ground can often be found. The irony is that languaculture at the level of shared human-ity becomes more important to "languacultural understanding" than the constraints that initially caused the task disruption. This might always have been true, at an intuitive level. In my travels over the years, I've always been impressed by how some people easily handle "cultural" differences while others rapidly make a mess of things. My experiences were mostly limited to observations of Anglo-American or European backpackers, busi-nessmen, and government people. I think it's because the successes easily ratcheted the level up from a problem with immediate local differences to common humanity.

And therein lies the Greek-tragedy nature of intercultural communica-tion, diversity training, and the like. Differences are made sense of in terms of templates that represent categories that are believed to include the task participants. Differences in the templates are presumed to explain task con-flict. However well-meaning the professionals and task participants might be, the strategy is like trying to fix a nuclear reactor with a Swiss Army knife, certainly in today's global society made up of hybrids. The template is very likely oversimplified and outdated. It might have some significance for participants. But what that significance means cannot be assumed; it has to be learned by an outsider. For hybrids, many other social influences, some of them contradictory, will also be part of their task languaculture.

So one kind of generalization that grows in importance with hybridity is how similar we all are. That's an incentive to learn—and keep learn-ing—as much as one can about universal humanity and about the global histories that shaped humanity. Perhaps a student could start out with something radical, like what they used to call a liberal arts education. Don't teach an outmoded version of the "culture" of a place where someone is going. Teach them about universal humanity together with ways to trans-late that knowledge into any local situation including those populated by hybrids. I know, I sound like Grandpa Abe Simpson writing one of his letters to the editor, but he was right once in a while.

To get clear on how to think about the universal/local mix of any languacultural moment, let me draw on some complexity theory, at least metaphorically. Nonlinear dynamic systems—the more accurate name for the theory—show how there are several kinds of change possible as a system moves through time.

One kind of change is Big Bang–like. It is called a *phase transition*. A system is no longer what it was before because of a relatively sudden reorganization; it has become a different kind of system. The change will be sudden, S-curve-like. The second kind of change has to do with what is called *path dependence*. The system doesn't change, but the path of a particular "run" varies from one time to another. Phase transition means new paths are inevitable; path dependency means that more than one path is possible but all possible paths will occur within the limits of what the system is capable of.

It's not just languaculture where this distinction between two types of change applies. Consider climate change: Weather is a path; climate is the system that defines the space within which those paths can occur. As the climate changes, new kinds of weather paths become possible. As another example, consider the 2008 economic depression: The financial system went through a phase transition with George W. Bush's financial reforms. As a result, home-buying mortgage holders and investment institutions traveled new and unexpected paths leading to financial disaster in the end for most everyone.

The Languaculture Big Bang was a phase transition. From it emerged generativity-driven innovations, constraints like naïve realism, and abilities like empathy. Within this new system, paths became possible that didn't exist before. But then, at any particular point on the path of any particular run of the system—different hunting-gathering bands each counting as a single run—the new universal abilities are still available as well. So a particular languaculture can use innovation to alter the course of a path *within* the new system that has made path innovation possible. And a particular languaculture can resist changes in that same path with constraint mechanisms like naïve realism dressed in local historical color. *Recursion*, the logicians call it. Generativity made the Languaculture Big Bang possible, but then generativity could also work in the context of any specific task.

So, no more capital C and L or small c and l. It's languaculture all the way down—a big change in system characteristics that makes different kinds of paths possible just because of those characteristics.

Mind as More than Just a Theory

Is there something in our common humanity that could help with the problem of handling hybridity? I've described how scholars of human evolution always mention culture and language as two critical features that made the Big Bang possible. They often mention other things as well. One of those other things has a peculiar name—*theory of mind*. I'm going to just talk about "empathy" in its place.

I can see some readers rolling their eyes at the thought of the touchy-feely nonsense to come, complete with a concluding chapter with suggested exercises for the involved parties requiring them to drop backward with their eyes closed in the hopes that the other person will catch them before they fall flat on their culture. No such thing. In this book, the concept means an ability—hypothesized as developing with the Big Bang—to build a mental model of another person's perspective based on what you know about them and the situation you're in.

I looked up *empathy* in my computer dictionary, but I liked the *Wikipedia* definition better: "Empathy is the capacity to understand or feel what another person is experiencing from within their frame of reference, i.e., the capacity to place oneself in another's position. There are many definitions for empathy which encompass a broad range of emotional states. Types of empathy include cognitive empathy, emotional empathy, and somatic empathy." A widely used quote by Alfred Adler, a founder of the school of individual psychology, describes empathy as "seeing with the eyes of another, listening with the ears of another, and feeling with the heart of another."

Just to remind the reader: Earlier I defined a *mental model* as one person's version of that "other being's frame of reference." We will call what that "other being" is using their *perspective* (whatever is required to make sense of the task and what actions they might take in it). Mental model, as noted earlier, will remain an outsider's term, the name for something an outsider makes up to identify *their* understanding of what another person's perspective is. You have a perspective. I have a mental model of your perspective.

So the working strategy for task-based languacultural conflict between two hybrids is this: How do we use this human ability—empathy—to correct our mental models of another person's perspective and make those models more useful (in the sense of getting the task back on track)?

Here is a classic example of the kind of experimental data that shows how empathy or theory of mind develops in humans, the famous Sally-Anne experiment (Wimmer & Perner, 1983). Sally and Anne are dolls in a dollhouse with no roof. Enter the experimental subject: a little kid. The experimenter reaches down, manipulates the Sally doll so that she picks up a ball and puts it in a basket. Now the experimenter walks the Anne doll away from the house so that she can't see what Sally does next. Sally then takes the ball out of the basket and puts it in a cupboard. The kid sees this happen. Now the experimenter brings Anne back into the house.

The question for the little kid is this: Where will Anne go to find the ball?

Until about age four, the little kid will answer that Anne will look in the cupboard. That's where the kid knows the ball is.

After age four, the little kid will answer that Anne will look in the basket. The kid knows that from Anne's perspective the doll is still in the basket because she did not see the transfer. The little kid has now acquired "theory of mind" ("empathy," I'm calling it here): the ability to build a model of how things might look from another perspective.

In a commentary that accompanied a study testing the ability of apes to ascertain the mental states of others, primatologist Frans de Waal stated that the claim that only humans have this capacity "is starting to wobble," complicating the human-animal boundary as he often does (2016). And, as in the earlier discussions of language, the secret rests in giving the primate an alternative system of communication. In the original Sally-Anne experiment, researchers monitored how the little kid with a theory of mind visually tracked the Anne doll when she returned to the dollhouse and looked in the wrong place. When the experimenters used eye-tracking software with nonhuman primates, their eye movement showed that they anticipated Anne's movements in the same way. They could figure out Anne's perspective as well. They just don't talk about it.

As usual, an ability awarded a major role in the emergence of *Homo sapiens* turns out to have clear precursors among animals. And, as usual, the emergence of human languaculture developed that ability beyond its earlier form. Empathy—at least a human version of it—grew as part of the Languaculture Big Bang. It names the ability to model the perspective of another person.

Perspective taking is a promising phrase to guide a new and different way to deal with human differences. Perspective taking happens when one person uses empathy to revise his or her mental model of another person's perspective. It requires working around whatever constraints are in the way by moving up in scale to universals, then using generativity to come up with alternatives to the initial model, trying an alternative out, revising, and continuing that loop until the task is back on track.

Successful perspective taking isn't just a mechanism to make hybrids happy with each other. It is also characteristic of con men, salespeople, politicians running for office, and interrogators. Social labels like that are more Machiavelli than Rousseau. Over the years I've seen references to a war leader like a general who obsessively empathizes with the enemy commander in order to figure out strategy for the next battle. Empathy isn't just for cooperation; it's also used to manipulate other people to one's self-serving ends.

At the moment I have in mind the more optimistic problem of mutual cooperation, where two or more people for whatever reasons want to work together to get something done. Nevertheless, manipulative uses for perspective taking might well be more frequent, and we'll return to them later.

"Perspective taking" sounds like a process based on the universal human ability for empathy, one that might be useful in figuring out a way to handle hybrid encounters that have run aground. It's a concept you find in psychology of the social variety, something we'll look at next.

A Little More Social Psych

The social psychology/social cognition field asks the same question that this book asks, though from a different angle of vision. The question goes like this: Now that we've shown how languacultures socially constrain individual perception and action, how do we explain the fact that those same people can rise above it, learn something new, and change their mental models of others? *Generate*, in a word. Like Boas said (if you recall his definition of culture cited in the first chapter), people can break the shackles of their tradition.

Some of that work goes by the name of *dual process*. It looks like an odd bit of jargon, and it has been overshadowed now by Daniel Kahneman's concept of fast and slow thinking (2013). The term *dual* just means that the theory explains how a mental model can both have its generativity and constrain it, too.

Dual means two. An example of the first process goes like this: The naïve realist rolls in with perspective intact and, based on just a few cues, knows what to do and how to do it. It resembles the efficiency of an episodic memory. Learning leads to habit and becomes an automatic part of languaculture. It acts as a constraint.

But the second process is very different: In this process, humans notice that things aren't working right, and the naïve realist stops, takes a look at what's going on, and comes up with something different that does work in the unexpected new situation. It requires more work and is more time-consuming.

That second kind of process should sound familiar. It is the generative process of analysis and combination that drove the Big Bang in the first place. Dual-process theories ask how and when that generative process is called on, in spite of all the constraint mechanisms that limit it.

The term *dual process* was coined by Marilyn Brewer (1988). She asked how it was that people—who normally use mental models automatically, top-down, without thinking about it—sometimes stop, pay attention, do some analysis, and come up with some innovation more tailored to the moment. How and why does that switch get thrown, the switch that changes levels, from normal, habitual naïve realism to the less typical analysis and learning and change? How do these two different processes, these dual processes, coexist with each other? How do they interact?

In a discussion of Martin Luther King's "Letter from Birmingham Jail" (1963), Moskowitz expands on some of the "key elements that contribute to . . . models of social cognition" (2005, p. 193). One is that this shift from naïve realism to generativity is caused by psychological tension (p. 194). Perspectives worn smooth by frequent use are supposed to make life easier, not more tense. Tension is a clear concept when it comes to coiled springs, but not so clear in the realm of perspective, especially considering that psychological tension might also cause retreat to a habitual perspective rather than to a change. In fact, that was the basic problem that Leon Festinger's (1957) theory of cognitive dissonance dealt with, another famous moment in social psychology. The tension between how one thinks the world works and one's perception of how in fact it is working gets to the point that one or the other has to change. In one famous example, whose source I can no longer remember, a member of the Flat Earth Society looks at a photograph taken from space and says, "You know, it's amazing how to the untrained eye the Earth looks round." (Google the society if you like; it's alive and well.)

What kind of psychological tension would cause a shift away from the tried-and-true perspective into something new? For Brewer, the answer is that it all depends on the actor's goals. Whatever those goals might be, tension reaches the breaking point when their perspective just isn't getting the job done. At a certain tension level—whatever "certain" means here—a person shifts to generativity to figure out what the problem is. Analysis and (re)combination come into play.

Moskowitz describes other theories, but these two—tension and goal frustration—are sufficient for present purposes. They do establish a couple of important things. They echo a theme of Moskowitz's book, and of social cognition more generally, that top-down processing is far and away the normal human approach to the world. It is the meat and potatoes of naïve realism.

But the theories also show that processing isn't always based on a habitual perspective, even when it is buttressed with all the constraint mechanisms described so far in this book. In order for generativity to take over, though, a person has to devote time and energy and attention to a problem. Something has to happen to knock the person out of deeply grooved habitual patterns, and then the person has to want to do something about it, and then something else has to happen so that the person changes their model, and then something has to make sure the person builds a better rather than a worse one. That's a lot of somethings.

At least the dual-process theories do show that habitual mental models can be brought to one's attention and analyzed and changed. It is possible, even if it doesn't happen often. It couldn't be all that frequent anyway, as both the evolutionary experts and the social psychologists point out over and over again, since stopping what you're doing and analyzing it and thinking up alternatives and trying them out. . . . Who's got the time? Not to mention that other people might think you're crazy (or a threat to society).

Whatever bright ideas anyone comes up with—ideas to reconfigure generativity and constraints to better serve our brave new global world—they can't require people to generate new perspectives every time the alarm clock goes off in the morning. The advantage of quick and automatic that gets us through the day needs to be preserved, or compensated for with some other advantage. Otherwise we'll all spend the rest of our lives lost in thought.

And Even More Social Psychology

Say a disruption in the middle of some task does call a person's attention to an out-of-awareness perspective they had been using. Tension rises and goals are blocked, like the theories claim. Say that a true dual-process moment occurs and is taken seriously with a motive to figure it out and change things. Now what? Does social psychology have any bright ideas about what to do next?

Yes, but the news isn't necessarily good. First of all, the field has a lot to say about how humans can use naïve realism to ignore the moment. The strategy is "blame the disruption on some other person involved in the task." In earlier writings I've called this the *deficit theory*—namely, the view that disruptions are caused by people who lack something. Maybe they do, sometimes, but it's not an assumption to be made without suspecting your own naïve realism.

Social cognition has obsessed for decades over this business of attributing what goes wrong to the other guy. Their jargon calls the obsession by the dramatic name of the *fundamental attribution error*. The concept means that an observer explains a problem situation in terms of another actor who is in it. They could explain in terms of characteristics of the situation, or even, god forbid, something they did themselves. But no, the overwhelming tendency is to look to another person to carry the blame.

Moskowitz describes many classic experiments around the theme of the fundamental attribution error. One of my favorites is the old Ross, Amabile, and Steinmetz (1977) quiz show exercise. Experts are asked to make up a question in some narrow area of expertise that no one outside their profession would ever know. Then the question is handed over to another person who plays the role of the TV host. The host asks the question of a person playing the role of contestant, who of course doesn't know the answer. Sort of a *Jeopardy* episode designed by a sadist.

So whose fault is it that the contestant doesn't know the answer? The task is loaded with reasons to explain how it was anything but the contestant's problem. It doesn't matter. Even though subjects in the experiment—the "audience" of the show—are told the entire story as I summarized it here, they still tend to rate the contestant as not too bright. And they rate the host, who didn't do anything but read the expert's question, as smarter than the contestant.

Is there any cure for the fundamental attribution error? Yes, there is. What if the subject of the experiment—the one doing the judging, the observer—is first asked to imagine that he or she is the contestant in the quiz show? Now, instead of rating another person, the subject is asked to explain him- or herself under the same circumstances.

The researchers didn't ask that question in the quiz show study. But they did in another famous experiment, the Snyder and Frankel (1976) sex tapes, which sounds almost as dramatic as the phrase "fundamental attribution error." A person is videotaped talking about intimate details of his sex life. Another person, the subject, watches the videotape of that interview. The interviewee acts anxious. The subject who is watching the tape explains the interviewee's anxiety by saying that this clearly is an anxious person.

Now suppose the subject who is watching the interview is asked to put himself into the same situation. Does he describe himself as an anxious person? Usually not. He concludes that of course he feels anxious: this stranger is asking him about his sex life—and videotaping him. Lucky for them it was such antique technology. I can imagine nowadays some mischievous student putting the digital files on YouTube.

This actor-observer difference means that, if subjects explain others by imagining themselves in the same situation, then the explanation tends to be in the situation, not in the person. If it's me who didn't know the answer in the quiz show, I give you all kinds of reasons why, like the way the whole game was loaded against me. If it's me who's nervous talking to a stranger about the intimate details of my sex life, then of course I'm a little nervous. The problem obviously isn't me personally. It's these researchers asking me inappropriate questions and videotaping my answers.

The phrase *actor-observer difference* is a bit of jargon that sums this up. The observer explains the actor with personal attributions. The actor explains him or herself with the situation.

I joke that the fundamental attribution error makes me think that social psychology is a Protestant social science. From my own Catholic background, and from conversations with Jewish friends over the years, I know of many cases where guilt overrides social theory and the actor in fact does explain his or her own mistakes with personal attribution. Maybe Baptists, too. "Through my fault, through my fault, through my most grievous fault," as we say during Mass. Note the repetition for emphasis. It sounds more benign in Latin, but it is not situational attribution in either language.

Jokes aside, and whatever the truth of them might be, observers who build a mental model of the perspective of others, who put themselves in the other's shoes, as the old saying goes—it looks like a strategy that might serve as an antidote to naïve realism. And it might be experienced less as a criticism and more as a game. Instead of "Maybe it's your mental model," it becomes "Pretend you're an X; what would you do?"

This premise is a cliché painted on tourist tchotchkes all over the American Southwest: "Before you judge a person, walk a mile in their moccasins." Ashtrays, coffee cups, you name it—the cliché is everywhere. Not that the waves of Indian, Spanish, and Anglo conquests tried on each other's footwear much historically. The cynical twist on the saying is more suited to the real story: "And after you walk, you'll have their moccasins and be a mile away." Talk about the dark side of empathy.

There is some hope in this idea of taking another perspective, though it won't be any panacea. One promising sign, though, is that the concept spins off in several interesting directions that aim toward practical strategies. Moskowitz cites several psychology deities who argue the value of taking another perspective. In a discussion of Fritz Heider's work on what is required to consider "the psychological world of the other person," Moskowitz says, "We must be able to stand in the shoes of others, see the world through their eyes, empathize with what they are feeling, and attempt to think and react to the world in the same way that they think and react to the world" (2005, p. 277). He sounds a little moccasin-like, but never mind.

In fact, even the most naïve of the naïve realists already knows how to model another perspective. Perspective taking developed as human societies became more complicated, as markets grew and specialized roles for craftspeople and religious and political specialists increased. People take on other perspectives as an ordinary part of modern life. Gallons of academic ink have been spilled over how parts of vocabulary represent different angles of vision on the same task. "Buy" and "sell" are two frequently used examples, two verbs that label the same task from different perspectives. Fillmore, the linguist whose case grammar was so useful in chapter 2, moved in this direction later with his *frame semantics*.

The ability to take another perspective is a human universal. But a naïve realist's mental model of other perspectives will be superficial at best and in service of their own interests. One person might believe they already know another's perspective. In fact, they might be arrogant about it when in fact it's just their naïve-realist fantasy. "No one understands these people like I do," said by an outsider, is a warning that, in fact, almost everyone else probably understands the insiders better. That's not the kind of perspective taking that can handle dynamic global diversity.

Other material from social psychology also flashes warning signals. For example, the famous Zimbardo prison experiment in 1971, mentioned earlier in this book. Students were locked in the basement of a university psychology department. Some students were assigned the role of prisoner. Others were assigned the role of prison guards. The experiment was closed down after six days. As Philip Zimbardo explained afterward, "We were horrified because we saw some boys ('guards') treat other boys as if they were despicable animals, taking pleasure in cruelty, while other boys ('prisoners') became servile, dehumanized robots" (Zimbardo, 1971, p. 3). This is perspective taking with a vengeance. Subjects in the prison study acquired a more profound sense of what it meant to be a guard and an inmate. Not to mention learning that college students from an elite university were capable of hatred and cruelty, in the case of the guards, and of humiliation and suppressed rage, in the case of the prisoners. My alma mater, too. I could have warned them—I went through fraternity rush.

Perspective taking doesn't guarantee a "they lived happily ever after" kind of ending. In fact, it might bring out the worst. But perspective taking also points in positive directions. In fact, Zimbardo is now a crusader who talks about the "Lucifer effect," as he calls his recent book (2007). In addition to looking at how situations can bring out our dark side, he looks at how they can bring out the hero in us. I haven't read the book, but based on his experiment, his concern with the tortures in Abu Ghraib, and the book's title, I can't help but think that the bad news is in the foreground.

But there are many positive examples as well. A therapeutic version of perspective taking is found in the work of Jacob Moreno, a Viennese man who moved to the United States in 1925 (2008). In Vienna he had experimented with storytelling—first with children, later with adults. He asked the storytellers to take on roles and act out the plots; then he extended these methods into "psychodrama," a therapy still with us today. (By the way, Moreno also created the "sociogram," a forerunner of the social-network theory described in the previous chapter.)

Psychodrama changes an observer into an actor. Role taking and role playing are key concepts. Group members act out different roles in an improvisational style, with the therapist called the "director" to support the theatrical metaphor. Moreno argued that psychodrama involved patients in their own therapy—an improvement, in his view, over their passive role in Freudian analysis. The approach continues today with a substantial following. (See http://www.asgpp.org/ for the American professional organization.)

Another application of perspective taking that comes to mind is the role-playing game (RPG). In fact, you could look at many social and psychological experiments as RPGs. RPGs have a long history. Dungeons and Dragons started the contemporary trend in 1974. I've never indulged, but a quick look at the web teaches that RPGs are less about competition and more about the collaborative building of a story through the character's perspective that each player takes on.

There is much to say about RPGs, including the more recent serious game movement, supported by an initiative of the Wilson Center Science and Technology Innovation Program (https://www.wilsoncenter.org/about-the-serious-games-initiative). The story about the work I did with others to develop the training game for Afghanistan is a classic example. In serious games you play to learn, whether the topic is urban warfare or health care or mediation of the Israeli-Palestinian conflict. Maybe an RPG to reorganize the relationship between generativity and constraints? I don't know enough about computer games, but the idea intrigues me.

Recently I helped run a workshop on complexity theory for Veterans Affairs researchers. It went pretty well, though at first the presentations were of the academic sort—well done, to be sure. An Australian colleague with experience in training practitioners suggested a game. Some of us groaned at the thought of the nonsense to come. But no. We were divided into different groups of stakeholders and instructed to interact with each other within and between groups to improve efficiency within the VA. Everyone got into it, and by the postmortem an hour or so later we were able to come up with several ideas about how the system worked—and didn't.

With my background, I of course noticed another major connection: the link between perspective taking and ethnography. Ethnography could even be defined as a means to the end of investigating, learning, and modeling a different perspective. Ethnographers are professional perspective takers. Think of ethnography as going from an outsider perspective to a model of an insider perspective. Think of the concept as a research version of perspective taking that's been around for a hundred years. Of course, a strategy for handling diversity that required everyone to be an ethnographer would be ridiculous. However, there should be some ideas in the research tradition that we can use.

When a concept like perspective taking is this productive, and this widely distributed across academic and practical fields, it's a good candidate for a useful universal. And if it's a universal, I can use it in this book to handle hybrid diversity in tasks.

Perspective taking is based on a human universal called empathy (or theory of mind, if you prefer). Generativity is something you can do with the information that results—namely, analyze and recombine. The game format, also a human universal, is a way to uncouple the problem from an immediate task and cast it in more general terms.

A long time ago, I was at another workshop in Jerusalem, this time for substance-abuse professionals. The news for this workshop—it was a big deal at the time, and probably still would be today—was that both Israelis and Palestinians were invited. Toward the end of the week, we all took a field trip to Yad Vashem, the Holocaust museum. The museum is powerful in its architecture and visual displays in conveying the horror of the

Holocaust. I had gotten to know a few Palestinians because we all smoked cigarettes during coffee breaks outside the conference, and a Palestinian colleague walked with me through some of the displays. He turned to me with moist eyes and simply said, "I had no idea." He knew, of course, that the Holocaust had happened, and he wanted an independent Palestine, and he had no love for the way Israeli authorities treated him and his neighbors. But still, the museum had been a perspective-taking exercise that he hadn't expected. I have no idea what (if any) long-term effect the experience had on him. But the power of the experience at the moment he had it was obvious, and it might have opened a window for him into a revised model of at least some Israeli perspectives.

A museum can be an "aha" moment for perspective taking. So can films, novels in translation, YouTube, the internet in general, and many other sources. The key is to get people out of the problem space and into a discourse space where they can use empathy to look at a task problem. A model for doing just that will be described in the next chapter.

Whatever the strategy that we make up for bringing about a powerful experience of perspective taking, we will need to put people outside the immediate task experience to get at the different perspectives that we want them to remodel. Museums and games and ethnographic research—not to mention films, web pages and stories of all kinds—have ways of doing that. So whatever ideas we come up with at the end of this book need to take that lesson seriously.

Social Perspective Taking   6

"**P**ERSPECTIVE TAKING" LOOKS LIKE the right name for what I'm after here. The concept names a skill that can kick in when problems with human differences surface in any task. It could be called a "metatask," a task available in the background to handle task problems. As the academic joke goes, "Anything you can do, I can do meta." To get started with the idea, I'm going to use an overview of social perspective taking (SPT) available on the internet courtesy of Digital Access to Scholarship at Harvard. The report, published in 2009, was sponsored by the US Army Research Institute for the Behavioral and Social Sciences. Here's how the concept is defined in the report:

> Perspective taking has been defined as a skill requiring a combination of cognitive and affective/emotional skills and the propensity or motivation to engage in the activity (Gehlbach, 2004). According to Gehlbach, perspective taking consists of the strategies we use to figure out what others are thinking and feeling and their perception about situations. Johnson (1975) also notes that perspective taking requires a kind of social awareness: "Taking the perspective of another person is the ability to understand how a situation appears to another person and how that person is reacting cognitively and emotionally to the situation. It is the ability to put oneself in the place of others and recognize that other individuals may have points of view different from one's own" (p. 241). Perspective taking goes well beyond that feeling of resonance between two people and is an explicit representation of the other, by means of the cognitive and emotional resources of the self. (Roan et al., 2009, p. 2)

For successful perspective taking, a person must also consider him- or herself as a source of distortion—naïve realism—that can be changed through experience to achieve a more accurate mental model of another person's perspective.

This is very much an empathy approach. In fact, the report also features a discussion of "empathy" but warns against "sympathy." Empathy requires that the perspective taker maintain agency—that is, autonomy, a sense of self separate from the task of understanding another. The purpose of SPT isn't to *become* the other; it is to improve one's ability to figure out where the other is *coming from*. Sympathy, by contrast, usually means emotional identification with another. Emotional engagement is required; emotional identification gets in the way.

I worked with the Army Institute many years ago during my brief but meteoric career with security forces. Their workshop, like the one I mentioned in chapter 1, was held during that brief moment of alliance between Obama and Petraeus regarding the naïveté of the United States about other parts of the world.

There are many stories to tell. One of my favorites involved the experiences of a captain assigned to run a small Iraqi town. He said he had no idea what to do. Over time, tensions and casualties increased. He decided, he told me, that he would try something different. "I'm going to run for mayor," he said. He increased his social visits, kissed babies (as far as I know), and did things that, according to his perspective, would give the impression that he was a friendly presence to be supported rather than a threatening one to be feared. He was a courageous guy, wandering through hostile territory without putting on full "battle rattle," as they called it. He said he didn't know how much to attribute to his change in behavior, but tension visibly lessened, and the casualty count on both sides went down.

Stories like his and arguments from a few visitors spun the workshop off in a new direction. Of course it makes sense to teach people something about a new place they're headed for, though "teach" is often thought of in a much too limited way. But the new direction we advocated was something like this: Complicated as our global world is, forget teaching what to expect in concrete tasks before arrival. Instead, teach what to do once you get there to learn what you need to know.

The idea was a dramatic departure from the traditional concept of intercultural training that originally drove the workshop. According to that model, you tell people what they're going to find, and off they go. The recent army report on perspective taking takes another argument as foundational: *Most of what you learn will happen after you arrive.* Dump the old model of "Here are ten facts about the place you are going. Memorize them and act accordingly." Remember the business card example from Japan? The army SPT report, in contrast, advocates a dynamic and engaged learning that develops over time, based on actual task experience.

The description of how SPT works is very much in the tradition of languaculture: "Important communication skills needed for SPT therefore includes active listening, checking for understanding by using nonverbal cues, paraphrasing and mirroring, and asking questions that verify SPT accuracy" (Roan et al., 2009, p. 9). However, there is a languacultural fly in this soothing SPT ointment. What if you—the newly trained perspective taker—are a native speaker of English and the other person in the disrupted task is not? If the fundamentals of shared phonology, morphology, and syntax aren't in place, the two task participants will not be able to get into the semantic and pragmatic space except via indexical and iconic signs. Even if the two can both structure mutually intelligible sentences, semantics and pragmatics will still cause problems. In some cases, a simultaneous interpreter may be required, which introduces numerous additional issues to task repair that this book cannot even begin to cover.

For instance, older readers will recall the famous moment when Nikita Khrushchev, premier of the Soviet Union during the 1950s and 1960s, announced to the West, "We will bury you." It was heard as a threat to conquer and kill. Younger readers can imagine what sort of international shock and awe that set off. As it turned out, the sense in Russian was a way of saying, "We (communism) will outlive you (capitalism)." Not quite the same thing. Or consider the famous, probably apocryphal, story about President Truman at a baseball game with the Japanese prime minister. The simultaneous interpreter listened to the president, turned to the prime minister, and said, "The president just told a joke. You should laugh."

This is the fatal flaw in the army report, and in much of the intercultural industry. SPT fits the general argument of this book pretty well so far. But it assumes that a common languaculture is available as far as the foundations go—or it requires a simultaneous interpreter.

Nonetheless, the report is eerily ethnographic. The SPT report is not meant to teach how to do ethnography. It is much more narrowly focused. It is aimed at completion of a specific task. But within that narrow focus, there are cycles of informal learning–testing–learning more and so on that resemble "ethnographic moments."

The report emphasizes that the perspective taker is not trying to become just like the other person; rather, they are trying to check out and improve their mental model of that other person's perspective. Obviously the perspective taker has to be motivated, emotionally engaged but not emotionally controlled, and willing to consider on reflection how their own perspective is part of the problem. The majority of the experts say case studies and role-plays are the best material to work with. There are many more details in the report, especially in the appendices.

The report boils down its advice to a four-step program. Here is the summary from the document:

> The proposed curriculum is designed to teach a four-step social perspective taking method that Soldiers can use in the field. . . .
>
> Step 1. "You don't know what you don't know" . . .
> Step 2. "Consider self, then other" . . .
> Step 3. "Check in" . . .
> > ° Communicating Through Questioning and Mirroring—the Soldier makes sure he or she engages in thoughtful inquiry, and parrots back to his or her conversation partner what it is he or she thinks they're saying.
> > ° Modifying Hypotheses as Needed—As the Soldier gathers additional information, he or she may change his or her understanding and estimation of the truth. Hypotheses are then rebuilt, if needed. . . .
> Step 4. "Invest in outcome" . . .
>
> Published and presented work on aspects of the four-step method confirms it helps to resolve conflicts and increase historical empathy, an understanding of how the past affects the present of a cultural group. (Roan et al., 2009, pp. 22–23)

SPT fits with the general argument so far, though it still focuses on face-to-face encounters—as does most of this book. And we're still dealing with a situation in which there is a small number of people, all of whom are motivated to cooperate in a task. Nonetheless, the SPT template does emphasize a shift from incompatible constraints that caused task disruption to collaborative use of generativity—analysis and recombination—to figure out how to repair task disruptions and get on with things. It foregrounds task rather than identity or culture as the main location of the problem. It leaves open the question of how to generalize the problem and the repair based on subsequent experience, so it accommodates hybrids. It doesn't require becoming something you're not. It emphasizes communication to become aware of and correct one's mental models rather than promising agreement on a solution, so it's different from negotiation or mediation. SPT won't necessarily resolve a conflict, but it will make it clear why it exists. And, in the process of correcting each other's mental models, SPT may well forge a new relationship among task participants that goes beyond and endures longer than the task itself.

One way of seeing SPT is that it's a way to modify a languaculture for a task when a disruption makes clear that the parties involved stumbled on a difference over just what that languaculture might be. Always assuming—once again—that everyone is motivated to restore cooperation and that everyone can structure symbols to communicate with each other.

So Why Did I Bother Writing This Book?

In the first two chapters I dragged the reader through the concepts of culture and language, both upper- and lowercase. I did this in part because, during my several years of experience working on projects, this is the way the concepts are used in everyday discourse. I also did it to work toward a more accurate sense of the concepts, ironically enough in a way that allowed us to eliminate the distinctions with which this book began. We ended up with a single concept of languaculture and an understanding that any attempt to model another person's perspective would involve both human universals and differences at the same time.

Other major moves along the way involved the concept of "hybrid." This means that social-classification systems decrease in importance as people in a global society are influenced more and more by numerous different sources. I doubt anyone represents in a straightforward way a single "culture" anymore in the old-fashioned sense of the term.

The resources from psychology—social, developmental, and cognitive—suggested "perspective taking" as a good way to think about understanding differences among participants in a task. To my surprise, I then found the report by the army on the Harvard database that seemed, in a general way, compatible with the flow that this book had developed.

This book suggests a general way of thinking about a perspective-repair strategy. Drawing on theory of mind—empathy—we can say that cooperation means that both people have a mental model of the other person's perspective that suffices for the two to engage in and conclude the task together. The assumption is that when there's a breakdown in the task due to the people involved, it's due to a failure in mental models that can be corrected with empathy and iterative communication.

The dynamic of the repair involves several universals in addition to empathy. Naïve realism will always be a major suspect as a barrier. By contrast, generativity—analysis and (re)combination—will be a major source of innovation that will guide each person in altering their mental models, trying the revisions out, and then altering them again until there is, hopefully, a shared languaculture for the task at hand.

But, in this book so far, and in the army report, and in many intercultural communication sources, the encounter is stripped down to one-on-one and face-to-face. And it is assumed that both task participants have an interest in a positive task outcome and are motivated to restore cooperation as a means to that end. Nothing has been said about power, or manipulation, or systemic issues. There has been nothing about tasks where the face-to-face is participants representing organizations under tight control by the organizations themselves. And there has been nothing about other forms of communication, like texts and emails and tweets and memos and archives.

In fact, if we take the stripped-down conditions seriously, it raises the question of "Why worry?" Two people engage in a task in which they both have an interest, two people who are motivated to overcome problems in order to complete it—do they really need theoretical grounding or professional help to resolve the problem and get on with it? Isn't that what any pair of people working together would do given those circumstances and interests and motivations?

Earlier, in chapter 3, those were the conditions used to explain why languaculture took off in the ancestral condition. Small groups after the Big Bang learned that cooperation was possible beyond anything imagined before. They faced basic needs in a harsh environment. So one argument might be, forget all the complications. Just restore the multiplex face-to-face of the ancestral condition, and the problem will take care of itself. Maybe—so would go this hypothesis—this just defines the limited circumstances where SPT works.

That argument is the rationale for the variety of "people to people" programs. I was an AFS—American Field Service—exchange student to Austria in high school. The organization was founded by former ambulance drivers from World War I. Horrified by the carnage, they baptized AFS with a motto from a Sanskrit proverb: "Walk together, talk together, all ye peoples of the earth; then and only then shall ye have peace." As snarky seventeen-year-olds, we thought the saying was a little hokey. But as I wrote this, I laughed, thinking that maybe I'd written an entire book justifying student-exchange programs. Fine—that alone would be worth it. I wrote a book, learned a lot, and landed in support of an experience that shaped my life, one that I wish every kid could have.

But there is a deeper principle here, an argument that a first step to resolve a task breakdown might just be to restore a feeling among task participants that they are members of the same hunting-gathering band, metaphorically speaking, known to each other through long association, faced with a common problem, ready to innovate in an adaptive way, socially linked with multiplex network ties.

Once you look around using this template, it's easy to find examples. A colleague in Santa Fe is one of the founders of the Creativity for Peace Camp (as reported in Dent, 2014). For three weeks in the summer, a group of adolescent girls—half of them Israeli, half of them Palestinian— spend time on projects together as well as just living and knocking around Northern New Mexico. The interested reader should look at the newspaper article for telling quotes about the good and the bad, but on the whole the girls evaluated the experience as positive.

Another example: NPR ran a feature on what was called the First Steps Community Cookout (Chapelle, 2016). It was held in Wichita, Kansas—a joint production of the local Black Lives Matter group and the police department. By all accounts (I saw other sources at the time as well), it was successful in the spirit of this book—namely, linking people together with the means to the end of connections that enabled corrections to mental models to start and, with any luck, continue.

Here's one more story that I remember from the long history of Israeli-Palestinian negotiations. Obviously peace hasn't worked out, but back in the day negotiations moved to an old castle outside of Oslo. Stories filtered out about how well the negotiations were going, explaining that the key was the informality that developed. One of the primary negotiators was Dr. Yair Hirschfield, sometimes referred to as the "architect of the Oslo Process." Here are a few excerpts from a contemporary *Washington Post* article about Hirschfield and his efforts (Blumenfeld, 1993):

> The dial turned toward casual. They started off in January wearing suits and ties, and ended with a Palestinian negotiating in his pajamas. . . .
>
> Here Hirschfeld's informality was not only endearing, but an asset. It helped make this channel work, while parallel attempts in other countries dried up. He was realistic, even skeptical, often uncertain if they would meet again. Yet his good-natured growl and rumbling laugh projected optimism. . . .
>
> He trekked with [the participants] through the woods, down to a lake at 3 a.m., trailed by Norwegian security agents. He peppered the air with jokes; his favorite: the one about the gigolo, a pair of boots and Catherine the Great.
>
> They all began to joke. They did imitations, of their leaders and of each other. They nicknamed Arafat and Rabin the grandfathers, Peres and Holst

the fathers, Beilin the son. They coded the United States "the big country" and Israel "the little country."

Palestine and Israel seem even further away from peace now than they did then, but the Oslo meeting was and remains a bright moment in a difficult ongoing story.

These three examples do show the presence of a pattern under three very different circumstances. And the pattern does show some resemblance to the argument in this section. Namely, one way to deal with task(s) conflicts among hybrids is to walk the participants back from the task to social conditions approximating the ancestral condition—small group, multiplex relations, repeated shared task involvement, development of reputation and shared interest, enough time to quiet naïve realism in order to turn up the volume on generativity.

Let me close on a personal note: A few years ago my cousin Don died in a freak bicycle accident. He was a truck driver who lived in the California Valley. We had gone to the same schools and were only a couple of years apart in age, so I knew a lot of the people at his funeral. They were mostly white working class. We stood around the keg of beer in the garage and talked. This was a world I grew up in. I was more comfortable there than I usually am at an academic conference. But it was also a world I'd lost touch with, PhD that I'd become.

I remember listening to them talk about their lives (once an ethnographer, always an ethnographer). Man, were they angry. They had been smashed by the 2008 recession after years of decline and felt disrespected and ignored by their governments, their employers, and the mainstream media. They were all on (if not over) the financial edge. They wanted to smash back—that was my interpretation of what I heard. Real men hit back. A few years later Donald Trump was the perfect "smash" candidate. I know this is a cliché of the unending parade of talking heads since the election, but still, in living ancestral condition color, it was a powerful perspective-learning experience.

Wall Street caused the recession, and they—not Main Street—were the main participants in and beneficiaries of the political maneuvers that followed. Wall Street recovered; Main Street did not. As far as I know, there were no ancestral condition–like events where Wall Street, Main Street, and the government spent some extended time talking things over. No camp, no barbecue, no conversations in pajamas. Just a "smash" of last resort after-the-fact.

Imagined Communities

So, maybe it's not so crazy, the idea that task breakdowns can best be handled by stepping outside the task and talking things over in more of an informal ancestral condition–like event. True, the examples in the previous section were at low levels of scale, involving very few people measured against the size of the populations that the participants represented. However, the argument of this book is that a few small events can generate a large number of possible new task models that will then diffuse widely in an S-curve kind of way if they are successful.

Another way to connect hybrids is Benedict Anderson's concept of the "imagined community" (2006). He was a political scientist who wanted to explain how a person could feel part of a community—in his case, the state—when in fact that person didn't have face-to-face interaction with most community members. In his theory the "community" was usually based on shared language and/or history. When I first learned about Anderson's work, I remembered Ulf Hannerz's (1992) concept of the "management of meaning," how the state manages content through its institutions, like the media, education, and so on.

For purposes of this book, I thought of "community" much more broadly than just the state. For example, the simple fact that participants work in the same task in different places creates a possible "community of practice" (Lave & Wenger, 1991). As another example, I was a scuba diver for many years. Whenever I met another diver I had never met before, we had a lot to talk about. Earlier in this book, I told the story about meeting someone else who had gone to Catholic grammar school before Pope John XXIII. We had even more to talk about than divers.

So, here's the argument: Among the hybrids engaged in a task, among the many social influences that shaped them separately, there might well be an overlap in one or more imagined communities. Remember the story about Muryama in Japan? Dinner worked out because we were both 1960s students and knew publishing. Such overlap might be a connection that could make all the difference in mutual goodwill to repair a task, an instant connection in the same "band" even though the people involved had never met before and came from different countries. The scorpion in this ointment is that I'm not sure how reliable this "instant" connection might be.

Some years ago I was asked by the National Institutes of Health (NIH) to travel to El Salvador to help write a proposal to support programs to get kids out of gangs. A senior member from the national security forces was also a member of the group—for me, a questionable character to keep an eye on. But . . . he was a scuba diver. We became friends and worked well together. The proposal was funded. Later I asked a colleague from the development office how the project was going. Not so good, she said. The cop had stolen the money.

That's an example of a problem with imagined communities. They do offer points of connection among hybrids. In that sense, they re-create an ancestral condition to some extent. But it won't always be clear what relevance the "community" connection has to the task that is the problem and focus. For the official from the state police, cooperation in completing the task was as important to him as it was to me. But the reason it was important to him was because he alone would benefit from the outcome.

The Really Big Problems

I wanted to pick a problem so big that it would put this book in its place, make it seem like rearranging deck chairs on the *Titanic* (an old expression I was recently reminded of when Stephen Colbert used it). So I thought about ISIS. At the time of writing this book, ISIS is an imagined community, its social network spanning the globe. It is most feared by outsiders in the West and elsewhere for its unpredictable terrorist attacks. In its 2016 report, the Pew Research Center wrote this based on surveys: "More generally, Muslims mostly say that suicide bombings and other forms of violence against civilians in the name of Islam are rarely or never justified, including 92% in Indonesia and 91% in Iraq. In the United States, a 2011 survey found that 86% of Muslims say that such tactics are rarely or never justified. An additional 7% say suicide bombings are sometimes justified and 1% say they are often justified" (Lipka, 2017). Obviously the vast majority of Muslims have nothing to do with terrorism.

ISIS appeared in an S-curve kind of way. Governments have intervened—as usual, late in the exponential part of the curve—by trying to slow down the unsettling ease with which ISIS recruits young people. (The rate is said to have slowed recently, though there was some evidence in early 2017 that the rate was increasing among younger kids.)

The main source countries surprised me. Here is a recent report summarized in the *Huffington Post*: "Muslim populations most likely to join ISIS are not in the Middle East or Africa. Rates of ISIS recruitment are highest in highly developed western countries, the ones with cultures you might least associate with radical Islam. The finding is consistent with several other studies that have found overwhelmingly negative views of ISIS in majority-Muslim countries" (Galka, 2016).

Scott Atran is an anthropologist who has probably worked more up close and personal with ISIS than any other researcher. The report I cite here summarizes his recent recommendations to the United Nations Security Council (2015). A video of his presentation is available at https://www.youtube.com/watch?v=qlbirlSA-dc ("Scott Atran: The Youth Need Values and Dreams").

My original naïve mental model of ISIS was too simple. It went "offer a stigmatized and marginalized young person respect, identity, community, and historical significance, and you will probably get their attention—at least for a while." Atran's work is much more elaborate and subtle than that, and, needless to say, his analysis is based on a great deal of diverse and elaborate data.

But there are some common threads. One is also a thread of this book—namely, use empathy (but not sympathy) to correct your mental model of another person's perspective. In fact, Atran opens his YouTube presentation with a story from the days when he worked for Margaret Mead. The first item on her teaching list was "Use empathy." He reviews some of the strategies to dissuade youth from joining ISIS and finds them empathy-free. By and large, they don't reflect any engagement with their audience. No SPT in sight. For example, one strategy is to place "counter-narratives" on social media—in other words, tell stories about ISIS's violence and brutality. It pretty much misses the point of what is going on from a young person's perspective when they consider joining up.

So where does Atran wind up? To my surprise, in the video presentation, he winds up talking about an organization called Seeds of Peace (http://www.seedsofpeace.org/). The "seeds" are young people from conflict-ridden areas; this program means to support their dreams for peaceful change. I was surprised at how the program starts: "Our leadership development model begins with a transformational camp session in Maine. The program shifts attitudes and perceptions and builds respect and empathy." We're back to the ancestral condition—small group, face-to-face, enough time to let multiplex links develop. But the camp is only the beginning; then the "seeds" are sent home to work locally with their age mates. According to their web page in early 2017, more than 6,400 "seeds" had been trained and returned to twenty-seven different countries, where they are engaged in more than forty peace-building initiatives. As they summarize their mission on their web page, "We equip exceptional youth and educators with the skills and relationships they need to accelerate social, economic, and political changes essential for peace."

I can't evaluate Seeds of Peace without more research. And I should remind the reader that my source is another anthropologist, so similar perspectives are in play. Still, he knows more about an ISIS perspective and its attractions for alienated Muslim youth than most. His conclusion—that a peace-oriented movement among that same demographic might engage them with just as much passion—it makes a lot more sense than a cost-benefit analysis put forth by non-Muslim adults who really have no idea of the perspective that might attract a young person to the movement in the first place. And, much to my surprise, the "seeds" start and develop with a return to ancestral condition–like situations, first in the training camp, and then upon return to the local setting. The case I picked to contradict the argument of this book turns out to support it.

But the argument has narrowed considerably on the way to SPT, especially given the global criticisms of the "culture" concept with which this book started. How about the high-level encounters, like the recent one where President Trump called the Japanese prime minister by his first name because he didn't know that name order is reversed in Japanese (instead of personal name/family name, it's family name and then personal name)? What about issues of power? As in the famous government template for community input, "Here's what we're going to do. Are there any questions?" What about all of the literature on the joys and perils of cross-cultural internet communication? What about what Atran calls "sacred values," where no negotiation is possible in the eyes of the perspective holder?

These are reasonable questions, given the critique of the use of the culture concept in chapter 1. But also reasonable guidelines for the concluding chapter to come. One conclusion of the book is just this: The public discourse that links "culture" with "problem" is hopelessly opaque and overgeneralized. "Culture problem" simply includes way too many different kinds of situations. In this book I have whittled away at the concepts to get to the foundation of one kind of a problem, one that lends itself to SPT. In our globally connected world of hybrids, one strategy for dealing with problems in human social variation does not fit all. In the next chapter, let's look at what we have and what we left behind.

SPT in Living Color 7

S OCIAL PERSPECTIVE TAKING isn't a remedy for all possible problems of intercultural communication, or diversity, or inclusion.
There isn't a single framework that will solve every problem of
human differences in a global society. However, examples in this book,
and the frequent use of the SPT concept over the years in several fields,
show how that idea keeps resurfacing. You can't keep a good concept
down. Remarkable here is how well it adapts to several arguments in this
book. A brief list of the conditions favorable to SPT will show how they
handle the problems with the culture and language concepts described in
the first two chapters.

1. Recall how this book opened with critiques of the use of the
   culture concept in contemporary discourse. SPT neatly sidesteps
   this problem. It does not require that people involved in SPT use
   any social labels whatsoever, either before or after the fact. Instead,
   it's about people trying to figure out and repair a task disruption.
   Categories of "culture" or "identity" are not prohibited, but those
   traditional starting points in "intercultural communication" are not
   required in order to "take another perspective." By now I hope the
   reader suspects that those a priori categories might well get in the
   way rather than help, especially as an initial naïve-realism strategy
   after a disruption occurs.

   However, nothing prevents a person from learning from experience and then generalizing with *other* kinds of categories not usually
   associated with "culture." For example, serving alcohol during a

meeting might be a problem for a person for any number of reasons—ex-alcoholic, religious belief, allergy, or personal distrust of box wine. And a lesson from several related SPTs might generalize in a way that's kind of "cultural" but not in a traditional sense. For example, at an international workshop I helped run in Canada, outrage developed over the dinner meal. I asked the organizer what had happened. "I've said it over and over," she told me, "if you're arranging an international dinner, avoid pork and milk." And imagine the additional categories for the bewildered new host in Santa Fe—paleo, vegan, gluten free?

In fact, SPT training includes what we might call the *anti-categorical imperative*. The link to Immanuel Kant will add an aura of intellectual panache. And the term will remind the user to avoid categories initially and, if they are used at all, to carefully specify just what the category means in the context of the task.

Years ago I did a project for a health-outreach program in Baltimore. The program had both black and white staff. Anticipating this book in ways I would never have suspected, one conclusion I nervously presented was this: The tendency was that if there was a problem, and if there was a black-white difference in the vicinity of that problem, then that difference would be used to explain that problem. True enough, often enough. But at other times the racial categories got in the way of general explanations in terms of such differing perspectives as community versus science priorities or what exactly the "care" in "health care" meant.

Category avoidance, at least initially, also opens lines for human-to-human contact rather than a "clash of cultures." One way of getting around problems, I've argued in this book, would be to go directly to human universals, where a connection across hybrids can always be made. The "anti-categorical imperative" aims SPT in this very direction.

2. A second condition for SPT is the recognition that we are dealing with *hybrids*. Recall that *hybrid* means that a person today is subject to social influences from all over the globe. The old idea of "culture" as family of origin plus isolated community assumes boundaries and a stability that no longer exist.

Hybridity can involve influences that are incompatible, if not downright contradictory, within a person as well as between them. This adds unpredictability to SPT, since the participants who want to use empathy to revise their mental model are probably not aware of the biographical mix that produced the hybridity in the perspective of another. Hybridity is another good reason why cultural and social categories should be put on the shelf in the beginning. Let the hybrids involved in the task that has been disrupted start with the disruption and spin off from there. If SPT eventually lands in a traditional or ad hoc general category, there is a "chain of evidence" that supports it that can also be questioned.

I've already told stories about hybridity in this book. Another of my favorite examples of a nontraditional category involves tourism. There is, in my experience, a correlation between popular tourist routes and presentations of a "traditional" culture. A colleague who was working in Thailand first pointed this out to me. Along easily accessible tourist trails, celebrations of traditional Thai "culture" could be found in abundance. A few miles off the trail, however, you would be more likely to find a villager in a Grateful Dead T-shirt. Or, another of my favorites, the Stanford Club of New Mexico—an alumni association—invited area grads to a feast day celebration at a Northern New Mexico Pueblo. Several recent graduates and current students were from the community. I spent some time talking with one of the current students. He came across as a frat boy in traditional Pueblo dress. He was a very nice kid, and you have to consider with whom he was talking—an old Anglo alum. But he was hybrid through and through.

3. A task focus also works well with the anti-categorical imperative. Rather than jumping from a problem to a social category, the focus keeps participants oriented to the same topic, one that they are all experiencing. Recall that the concept of task also anchored the referent of "languaculture." "Task" assumes that participants want a shared way of cooperating to get it done. That shared way is the joint languaculture for the task that the participants create. The disruption in the task emerges from some part of languacultural differences in "perspectives." The purpose of SPT is to explore and clarify how those differences in perspective are modeled by participants and revise the models, whatever their origin.

For most of this book, I have focused on a single task with two participants. So does the army report. So did our serious game for Afghanistan, described in chapter 1. The problem is that in the real world, there may be more people involved and more than a single task in play. The fact that "no task is an island" creates problems.

For example, the task may be part of a larger task. Or a task may consist of many subtasks. Or a sequence of tasks may have many crisscrossing dependencies. Or the way that the task is accomplished may be so central in the perspective of one participant that change is all but inconceivable. It might link to a sacred value, or be so habitual that it is difficult to recognize. The communication that SPT initiates should lead participants as they interact into the relevant parts of the larger task structures.

As an example, consider the work I once did for an outpatient chemotherapy clinic. The original task focus was to get patient treatment underway in the shortest time possible. One important example of a task dependency I learned right away: if another patient experienced an emergency during chemo administration, everything stopped until the emergency was resolved. As another example, if a patient's blood test on arrival showed new clinical information, then the order to the lab would be delayed, and so would the treatment. I was led to these and other task-dependent parts of the work by the original task—reduce waiting time for patients. It emerged rather than being imposed with a prior category of person. The assumption is that SPT, like the clinic work, will lead task participants in new and different directions, often unexpected.

4. When I wrote the early chapters of this book, I had a peculiar idea, tongue-in-cheek, that maybe a return to hunter-gatherer conditions was the answer to the hybridity of global society. With time, my tongue left my cheek, especially when—as the reader saw earlier in selected examples—it turned out that there were some SPT success stories that supported the idea.

What exactly did I mean by a return to the ancestral condition? I meant the hypothesis that SPT would go better in a small group given the time to develop a shared history and reputations for trust and multiplex network ties. Initially I thought that this would limit the use of SPT. The alternative hypothesis is now that SPT is the best way to handle many situations and therefore task disruptions need to be dealt with in small groups. Later, successful small group repairs require diffusion to a larger population by other means, but that raises other issues and requires different kinds of modeling. I have no way of testing which hypothesis is correct. I can say I started the book betting on the first and finished the book betting on the second.

I found further support for my bet in the "two pizza" rule of Jeff Bezos, the founder of Amazon. The rule says that the upper limit on size for a productive meeting is the number of people you can feed with two pizzas. And, even as I wrote this, I learned about the Virtual Dinner Guest Project, in which two small groups linked by Skype sit down to a meal in their respective locations and converse over dinner (Wija, 2017). What could be more hunter-gatherer-like and universal then "breaking bread together," even if done digitally rather than with a campfire?

There you have some conditions for a successful SPT. The anti-categorical imperative, the assumption of hybridity, the task focus, and the use of participants in small numbers that can form a group more like a hunter-gatherer band. Even with this scenario, how does SPT proceed?

I'll start with a new numbering system now because I'm shifting from a list of conditions favorable to SPT to a number of steps and roadblocks as they are put into play in the process of using it.

1. Know that naïve realism—including its many manifestations, like out-group stereotyping, the fundamental attribution error, and so on—is a universal human-constraint mechanism.
2. Know that your mental model of another's perspective will be distorted by your naïve realism, but also know that that distortion can be corrected.
3. Use empathy. Understand that empathy refers to a universal human ability to model another person's perspective based on knowledge from and of them and the situation that you're in. It is not sympathy. It does not mean you want to become the other person, nor does it mean that you agree with them. It means that a person did something unexpected given your mental model of their perspective. As a result, you now want to use empathy to correct your model so that what originally was unexpected is now part of your expectations for what that other person might do.
4. From this point forward, SPT is interactive among the participants in the task. It requires communication among them. The problem must be "topicalized," as they say in pragmatics. That is, participants must shift from doing the task to talking about the problem that interrupted the task—the metatask. Ideally, everyone is committed to a cooperative outcome and stands to benefit from it. It is here

especially that the resemblance to ethnography appears, also noted in the discussion of the army report. There will be questions and answers, paraphrases, requests for clarification, and other tests of what the perspective taker thinks they know. All participants are motivated to continue the task, presumably because all will benefit as they did before the task was disrupted.

5. Under non-ideal conditions, another metatask comes into play—conflict negotiation, arbitration, mediation, or an imposition of will by some participants on the will of others. This is also where "sacred values" create the most formidable boundary of all.

When I lived and worked in New York City years ago, everyone thought I was Jewish. White guy with a PhD and a beard working on a social problem living on the Upper West Side near the famous deli Zabar's—it triggered something like an episodic memory among most people I met. I learned a lot of Yiddish. As George Carlin said, "I grew up in New York City, and I was sixteen before I found out that I wasn't Jewish." So I decided to learn about being Jewish. My colleagues were willing and amused teachers.

My friend Manny invited me to his son's bris. After he opened the front door to his home, he hesitated a moment, and then said, very politely, "Would you mind putting this on?" He held out a white yarmulke. I think he was being careful in case he was approaching a sacred Catholic value. Of course I put on the yarmulke. Manny said, "You look just like the pope."

But it could have been trouble. Any signifier that links to a sacred signified—however trivial from the outside looking in—it might have a nuclear effect on a task. Consider headscarves in the case of Muslim women. Some Western European countries argue about whether it should be illegal to wear them in public. The issue has become particularly volatile since the scarf can signify a sacred value from both perspectives: piety on the one hand and a woman's freedom on the other. And "public" labels a very large number of tasks where disruption might occur—a recipe for multitask disaster.

However, a colleague did her dissertation work with discussion groups in Israel among Jewish and Palestinian neighbors. She was a languaculture type, so she focused on the communication patterns (Zupnik, 1995). When the topics were the everyday tasks of urban life (those that everybody had to deal with), in spite of the fact that these tasks went differently depending on whether the storyteller was Jewish or Palestinian, conversations were lively and cooperative.

I don't know whether these groups continue to this day. A story on NPR in 2017 featured something similar where Israelis and Palestinians in the same neighborhood were also learning each other's languages (Kakissis, 2017). Such groups represent another example of the kind of people-to-people, back-to-the-ancestral-condition strategies that might make SPT more likely to succeed.

The topic of sacred values is a good place to finish this book, with a brief discussion of the possibilities and the limits of the arguments for SPT.

Round Up the Usual Hedges

I'm not sure when "world peace" became a cliché. It might've been that bumper sticker that called for "whirled peas." It connotes an idyllic state, like most utopian fantasies. Professions like intercultural communication or diversity training often assume that communication can solve any conflicts that might arise. Reasonable people can agree on common ground acceptable to all once it is discovered by talking things over.

The sociologist and philosopher Jürgen Habermas offered a theory that represents this position. He called it *universal pragmatics*: "The task of universal pragmatics is to identify and reconstruct universal conditions of possible mutual understanding [*Verstandingung*]. . . . Other forms of social action—for example, conflict, competition, strategic action in general—are derivatives of action oriented toward reaching understanding" (1976, p. 1).

He goes on to describe how this consensus might be reached. What is said must be true, must conform to local norms, and must represent sincere intentions on the part of the speaker. The first problem is that the list of conditions that must hold are also sources of differences in perspective that might be in need of repair. The second problem, already mentioned, is that "understanding" does not necessarily mean "agreement." The third problem is the potential impermeable membranes around the task—sacred values and power differences have been mentioned in this book. The fourth problem is scale, one that has come up frequently in this book—the fact that most work focuses on face-to-face encounters. What about larger-scale problems?

Habermas offers a consensus model for differences in perspective, one where everyone has equal rights to the floor, where the final repair will be a consensus, and where everyone will say only things that are sincere and truthful. It reminds me of an academic version of Rodney King's cry in the wilderness: "Can't we all just get along?" That, like universal pragmatics, has become an example of naïveté.

Academic anthropology is also famous for its naïveté, and that is the tradition that shaped my perspective. Consider the example of President Obama: Many people don't know that his mother was an anthropologist and that he grew up in part "in the field" in Indonesia. Anthropology has a bias in what the job entails, a bias that I represent as much as his mother did. We investigate a variety of perspectives and build models to show how all those different perspectives are interrelated.

It's no surprise that Obama became a community organizer to apply what he learned at his mother's knee. And it was no surprise (to me, at least) when I watched him, during his first two bulletproof years with a Democratic Congress, waste his time trying to build a consensus in Washington. He was just doing what came naturally to him or anyone else under the influence of anthropology. It took him until the last two years of his term (in my opinion as a twenty-year resident of that peculiar city) to figure out that Washington was about power, not consensus.

All of this is by way of offering a "perspective" on this book. As the old saying goes, I learned to "cut the cloth to suit the coat." Or, as a particularly bloodthirsty consultant put it, "cut the patient to fit the table." I started out thinking that everyone out here in the world is tossing around the concept of culture like a beach ball. Culture has been at the center of anthropology for more than a century. Therefore, I should be able to help straighten this out and make the concept useful.

This book turned into a conversation between me and a lot of other sources, including other social and biological sciences, computer science, and complexity theory. I worried about covering so much sophisticated material for a general audience. I still worry, mainly because much of the biology was new to me and many changes in the conventional wisdom are underway. But, in the end, I think this book lays out a general content map of the territory that may help with—at least some of—the problems of conflict among hybrids in our global era.

But I worried about being naïve with any solutions I came up with.

I wanted to be sure that I didn't pretend that the entire problem would yield to my anthropologically inspired argument. No whirled peas. Logically enough, though, the anthropological compass led to a look back at the beginning of culture and language, and then a look forward at what the world had turned into since then. The idea was that maybe there is a link between the origins and the current breakdown in our ability to handle human differences. Maybe the link would inspire some new strategies.

The first link was obvious: The sociobiological world where languaculture developed was dramatically different from the sociobiological world of today. As a result, social influences that shape a person's identity now flow in from numerous different sources across the planet. This meant that monocultural labels that might have described hunting-gathering bands would no longer work in a straightforward way. As this book developed, I began using the term *hybrid* more and more. Task disruptions are more likely to occur among hybrids now.

The second link was the close tie between language and culture—languaculture—and task. The change that this link inspired was to stop using *languaculture* as a coherent and comprehensive general label for person or group. Now it can be used as a term for the tacit knowledge that allows two or more people to work together in at least one task. "Task" can have a minimum value of one and a maximum value of all the tasks that those two people do together. At the maximum value we approach the ancestral condition.

A third link was to focus on human universals that appeared with the Culture Big Bang. Particularly important here were innovations that come with generativity, constraints like naïve realism, and the ability to model another person's perspective with empathy. Universals help deal with the unexpected languacultural matchups that hybrids bring to a task without having to worry about what a priori social or cultural labels might or might not be relevant.

Promising as all this may sound, application raises several questions. The first is a question of scale. From the samples used in this book, it really does look like successful social perspective taking works to the extent that the task repair occurs in a context that resembles the ancestral condition more than the usual day-to-day of global life. The general idea is to get a small number of people on both sides of a task (or tasks) conflict, put them in a context where networks can become multiplex, keep it in informal mode, and see if the shift from uniplex to multiplex participation doesn't move the group toward repair of the original task (or tasks) that created the problem.

Success at this lower level can then scale up through diffusion. There is an organizational concept called *positive deviance*. It means that in a large organization with a problem, there will be a small group or two who have figured out how to solve it, usually by breaking the rules. So the advice to the organizational consultant goes like this: Find the positive deviants who have figured it out. Document what they did. Take it to the top, and advise them to distribute it. Maybe SPT has to be low scale in its creation. But successful efforts can diffuse more widely.

SPT is still bogged down by some serious assumptions. The most important one is that task participants are motivated to repair the problem and return to cooperation. This can get tricky. Power differences as reflected in control of resources will give the powerful participant more of a say in what counts as a satisfactory repair. Sacred values might also present insuperable barriers.

I think—with empathy—of the clerk in a small town right after the Supreme Court recognized same-sex marriages. She refused to issue licenses. Interviews in the media allowed her to explain that this was a sacred value for her. She could not support such marriages without denying her religion. But power required her to do just that as a condition of employment. Power neatly solved the problem by assigning the task to other clerks. No SPT work involved there. Power dodged a sacred value bullet.

Then there's the communication part. Recall the discussion in chapter 2 where I wondered about the mix of things usually considered "linguistic" and other things usually considered "cultural" in the concept of "languaculture." Though the boundaries blur at every level, it seems clear that phonology, morphology, and syntax—when compared to semantics and pragmatics—are more oriented to structuring the explosion of symbols that made human speech possible. Obviously SPT task participants must be capable of structuring languaculture in mutually comprehensible ways. Task performance and SPT that relies only on English gives a native English speaker home-field advantage. The "simple" answer is just to use an interpreter. The *just* in the previous sentence is the understatement of the century, given how difficult and subtle tacking the uncertain hybrid seas between languacultures actually is. A recent popular book provides a good nautical chart of translation for the interested reader (Bellos, 2011).

The moral of the story? Straightening out problems that come up when hybrids share tasks is loaded with contextual factors that limit the choices for an effective response. As I wrote this book, the trail I hacked through the new material and old experiences led me to SPT. It had a venerable history and spanned many disciplines and practices. It allowed me to connect the Languaculture Big Bang and contemporary global society. It does not require—but neither does it prohibit—use of general social and cultural categories, though the anti-categorical imperative cautions against them. And SPT fits the biases of the field, anthropology, that has long featured similar processes of modeling a different perspective. If the conditions to make SPT work are not present, then either those conditions must be created or some other approach must be used.

Adiós

I've always had trouble writing a conclusion. A book is its own conclusion. If nothing else, I hope the reader who made it to the end will never again say or see the word *culture* without wondering what it means. Thinking about what it means—with SPT as the guide—requires suspicion of general cultural and identity labels, questions about the specific task(s) where the problem arose, and the ability to communicate about the problem among participants.

And I hope that readers will think about the "language" in *languaculture* as well as the "culture" part. The culture mavens often talk about "communication," but that term is much too vague and ambiguous to handle the subtle details by which humans conduct and discuss their tasks. The communication that became possible with duality of patterning enables a rich system for structuring symbols. Phonology, morphology, syntax, semantics, and pragmatics build on earlier hominin and animal communication but exceed it in complexity and capacity. In fact, absent some shared fundamentals in symbol structuring, SPT couldn't work at all. A simultaneous interpreter would be required, a change in the SPT template that introduces all kinds of new issues that are only hinted at in this book.

A second hope is that a reader might try a little SPT for him- or herself. It doesn't have to be around a problem in a task in which you are a participant, though it could be. For example, you could have gone to the lowrider exhibition at the New Mexico History Museum and learned something—especially if you're a guy who grew up with cars—to revise your mental model about what a car can mean. Or you could buy a novel in translation by a person and from a place that you're unfamiliar with. There are many ways to experiment with SPT. I think it makes life more interesting, but then I would, since I've done it for a living most of my life.

A third hope—dream, really—is that some readers might find the SPT version described here worth some support or time or both. This book described an SPT concept, though limited in scope, that has promise. Social scientists talk about an "existence hypothesis." Certainly there is enough in this book to demonstrate the existence of one kind of SPT that looks promising. But to really make the case, an analysis of failed SPT is in order, as well as an evaluation of the staying power of its results. I haven't done either of those things here. The army/Harvard report described in chapter 6 reviews some material that supports positive answers to those questions, though.

It's not always easy to think in terms of SPT rather than traditional social and cultural categories. An acquaintance who is a professional mediator told me a story about a negotiation in the mountains outside of Santa Fe. The problem was the "enviros" versus "la gente." The task was to come up with a collective plan for use of public lands. The "gente" were the "people"—the Hispanic population of the region whose history contained the fact that these "public" lands were their common property before the American takeover in 1848. The environmentalists were concerned with the preservation of natural spaces. They talked in terms of "stewardship," easily heard as a claim to control of the land. There was plenty of hybridity on both sides, but in this case shared history defined strong racial boundaries—the visible kind, white and brown—that impeded the task. I asked my acquaintance—a brown person—why they had not come together around the fact that both sides might agree that the main purpose of the plan was to block commercial development. Apparently it didn't happen. I wonder whether this event might have benefited from a little SPT.

At any rate, SPT is designed for use by people without a required background in the academic knowledge that produced it. It is one of the few attempts to bridge theory and practice that looks promising for one large class of problems in "intercultural communication." And it responds to the origins of languaculture as well as its problematic fit with contemporary global society.

But Is It Anthropology or What?

Frameworks from anthropology are of increasing interest—witness the explosion of use of the culture concept to which this book responds. But the profession developed a languaculture over the decades that is one of the most opaque in the land.

For me, the first indication of a problem came with a presidential panel at the national anthropology meetings in the 1980s. The panel's charge, apparently, was to straighten out what culture "really" meant in the face of what was already growing interest in the concept. The panel basically deconstructed the concept and said, "Get back to us in a few years." This won't do.

In my view, we are all on an S-curve ride into a *post*-disciplinary age. Try this thought experiment, actually a choice now imposed on students who try to match training offered at the traditional university with theory, application, and practice relevant to something they'd like to do. The thought experiment goes like this: Pick a problem you'd like to work on. I'll bet people you find who work on that problem today have backgrounds from all over the traditional academic and professional map. *Interdisciplinary* used to be the word to describe such situations, but that older term is still about discipline. A better word is *transdisciplinary*, going beyond the old disciplines into a new space where new knowledge and practices can be created based on several different perspectives. But then what happens to the old disciplines, cemented as they are in academic bureaucracies, professional associations, journals, and so forth?

When I'm asked how I think this will all play out, I usually just shrug my shoulders and order another drink. What I really think is happening is something like this, and not just with anthropology. New patterns will continue to emerge. The patterns will work like this: Pieces of traditional disciplines X, Y, and Z will prove to be more effective and intellectually interesting in collaboration with each other when compared to how those pieces fare in the context of their home discipline. This has already begun and is happening now.

Then what happens? X, Y, and Z are given a new name, and new programs, institutes, and labs arise to meet the need. One famous example that will be familiar to many readers is a field we now take for granted—"cognitive science." When I was a grad student in the late 1960s and early 1970s, the headquarters for linguistic anthropology at Berkeley was the Language Behavior Research Laboratory, in its own house on Piedmont Avenue. To my surprise, there were also faculty from other departments that had to do with communication and cognition. It was in fact one example of the beginning of the new disciplinary configuration that would come to be called "cognitive science." Here's a brief blurb from *Wikipedia*, though it leaves out the important role of dedicated funding by the Sloan Foundation, as in money talks and bullshit walks. Nothing like an infusion of cash to turn that first inflection point in the S-curve:

> The term *cognitive science* was coined by Christopher Longuet-Higgins in his 1973 commentary on the Lighthill Report, which concerned the then-current state of Artificial Intelligence research. In the same decade, the journal *Cognitive Science* and the Cognitive Science Society were founded. The founding meeting of the Cognitive Science Society was held at the University of California, San Diego in 1979, which resulted in cognitive science becoming an internationally visible enterprise. . . . In 1982, Vassar College became the first institution in the world to grant an undergraduate

degree in Cognitive Science. In 1986, the first Cognitive Science Department in the world was founded at the University of California, San Diego.

I eventually left the cogsci fold, as did some others, as the new field became more and more computational and experimental, those emphases being interesting to me but peripheral to ethnographic research. Some disciplines were more "trans" than others. Though god knows, as readers can see in this book, I learned to use experimental data and computational thinking as part of my work. Still, the cognitive science story is an early example of what I see going on around me more and more as categories and practices shape-shift from traditional disciplines to new transdisciplinary configurations.

SPT is most emphatically not anthropology in the traditional sense. But, as I learned in the course of writing this book, it is certainly compatible with fundamentals of traditional anthropology; it certainly enables a mix of disciplinary, professional, and practical perspectives; and it is intellectually interesting and urgently needed in our contemporary world. There's plenty here to criticize and improve, and research more. But it makes me happy that, finally, I think I've learned how to write a transdisciplinary book.

References

Agar, M. (1994). *Language shock: Understanding the culture of conversation*. New York: William Morrow.

Agar, M., & Reisinger, H. S. (2002). A tale of two policies: The French connection, methadone and heroin epidemics. *Culture, Medicine and Psychiatry, 26,* 371–96.

Alfred, K. (n.d.). Monkeys washing potatoes: Do animals have culture? [Blog entry]. Retrieved from http://alfre.dk/monkeys-washing-potatoes/

Anderson, B. (2006). *Imagined communities: Reflections on the origin and spread of nationalism*. London and New York: Verso.

Asch, S. E. (1951). Effects of group pressure on the modification and distortion of judgments. In H. Guetzkow (Ed.), *Groups, leadership and men* (pp. 177–90). Pittsburgh, PA: Carnegie Press.

Atkin, A. (2013). Peirce's theory of signs. *Stanford Encyclopedia of Philosophy.* E. N. Zalta (Ed.). Retrieved from https://plato.stanford.edu/archives/sum2013/entries/peirce-semiotics/

Atran, S. (2015, December). Response to a request for recommendations to the UN Security Council Committee on Counter Terrorism. *Journal for Risk Assessment, 3*(12). Retrieved from http://www.jpolrisk.com/response-to-a-request-for-recommendations-to-the-un-security-council-committee-on-counter-terrorism/

Austin, J. L. (1975). *How to do things with words*. Cambridge, MA: Harvard University Press. (Original work published in 1962)

Bateson, G. (2000). *Steps to an ecology of mind: Collected essays in anthropology, psychiatry, evolution, and epistemology*. Chicago and London: University of Chicago Press. (Original work published in 1972)

Bellos, D. (2011). *Is that a fish in your ear? Translation and the meaning of everything*. New York: Faber and Faber.

Bergmann, J. R. (1987). *Klatsch*. Berlin: de Gruyter.

Blumenfeld, L. (1993, September 22). The absent-minded miracle worker. *Washington Post*. Retrieved from https://www.washingtonpost.com/archive/lifestyle/1993/09/22/the-absent-minded-miracle-worker/888a485a-2fb1-4c33-a51c-c7ade1dc5904/?noredirect=on&utm_term=.f3e000d2d4d4

Boas, F. (1974). *A Franz Boas Reader: The Shaping of American Anthropology, 1883–1911*. G. W. Stocking Jr. (Ed.). Chicago: University of Chicago Press.

Bohannan, L. (1966). Shakespeare in the bush. *Natural History, 75*, 28–33. Retrieved from http://www.naturalhistorymag.com/editors_pick/1966_08-09_pick.html

Boyd, R., & Richerson, P. (1985). *Culture and the evolutionary process*. Chicago: University of Chicago Press.

Brewer, M. B. (1988). A dual process model of impression formation. In T. K. Srull & R. S. Wyer (Eds.), *Advances in social cognition, vol. 1* (pp. 1–36). London: Lawrence Erlbaum.

Brown, D. E. (1991). *Human universals*. New York and London: McGraw-Hill.

Burke, K. (1966). *Language as symbolic action: Essays on life, literature and method*. Berkeley: University of California Press.

Burling, R. (2005). *The talking ape: How language evolved*. Oxford: Oxford University Press.

Canclini, N. G. (2005). *Hybrid cultures: Strategies for entering and leaving modernity*. Minneapolis: University of Minnesota Press.

Chapelle, B. (2016, July 19). Police and black lives matter hold a cookout, and praise rolls in. *The Two-Way: Breaking News from NPR*. Retrieved from http://www.npr.org/sections/thetwo-way/2016/07/19/486581466/police-and-black-lives-matter-hold-a-cookout-and-praise-rolls-in

Chomsky, N. (1957). *Syntactic structures*. Berlin: Mouton Gruyter.

Cohen, M. D., March, J. G., & Olsen, J. P. (1972). A garbage can model of organizational choice. *Administrative Science Quarterly, 17*(1), 1–25.

Corballis, M. C. (2003). *From hand to mouth: The origins of language*. Princeton, NJ: Princeton University Press.

Dawkins, Richard. (1976). *The selfish gene*. Oxford: Oxford University Press.

Dent, M. (2014, July 24). Camp aims to build understanding between Palestinian and Israeli girls. *Santa Fe New Mexican*. Retrieved from http://www.santafenewmexican.com/life/teen/camp-aims-to-build-understanding-between-palestinian-and-israeli-girls/article_dd0fdcca-ceed-5cf5-a9ac-b72873f0a192.html

de Waal, F. B. M. (2016). Apes know what others believe. *Science, 354*(6308), 39–40. doi: 10.1126/science.aai8851

Diamond, J. M. (2006). *The third chimpanzee: The evolution and future of the human animal*. New York: Harper Perennial. (Original work published in 1992)

Donald, M. (1993). *Origins of the modern mind: Three stages in the evolution of culture and cognition*. Cambridge, MA: Harvard University Press. (Original work published in 1991)

Dunbar, R. (1996). *Grooming, gossip, and the evolution of language*. Cambridge, MA: Harvard University Press.

Eggan, F. (1963). Cultural drift and social change. *Current Anthropology, 4*, 347–55.

Everett, D. L. (2012). *Language: The cultural tool.* New York: Vintage.

Festinger, L. (1957). *A theory of cognitive dissonance.* Stanford, CA: Stanford University Press.

Fillmore, C. J. (1968). The case for case. In E. Bach & R. H. Harms (Eds.), *Universals in linguistic theory* (pp. 1–90). New York: Holt, Rinehart & Winston.

Fitch, W. T. (2010). *The evolution of language.* Cambridge: Cambridge University Press.

Fox, R. G. (1969). "Professional primitives": Hunters and gatherers of nuclear South Asia. *Man in India, 49*, 139–60.

Friedman, T. L. (2005). *The world is flat: A brief history of the twenty-first century.* New York: Farrar, Straus & Giroux.

Friedrich, P. (1989). Language, ideology, and political economy. *American Anthropologist, 91*(2), 295–312.

Galka, M. (2016, April 27). New research shows ISIS recruitment driven by cultural isolation. *Huffington Post.* Retrieved from http://www.huffingtonpost .com/max-galka/new-research-shows-isis-r_b_9782022.html

Geertz, C. (1973). *The interpretation of cultures: Selected essays.* New York: Basic Books.

Gehlbach, H. (2004). A new perspective on perspective taking: A multidimensional approach to conceptualizing an aptitude. *Educational Psychology Review, 16*(3), 207–34.

Goodenough, W. H. (1957). Cultural anthropology and linguistics. In P. Garvin (Ed.), *Report of the seventh annual Round Table Meeting on Linguistics and Language Study* (pp. 167–73). Washington, DC: Georgetown University Press. Retrieved from https://repository.library.georgetown.edu/bitstream/ handle/10822/555451/GURT_1956.pdf

Grice, H. P. (1975). Logic and conversation. In P. Cole & J. L. Morgan (Eds.), *Syntax and semantics 3: Speech acts* (pp. 41–58). New York: Academic Press.

Habermas, J. (1976). *Communication and the evolution of society.* T. McCarthy (Trans.). Boston: Beacon Press.

Hannerz, U. (1987). The world in creolisation. *Africa: Journal of the International African Institute, 57*(4), 546–59.

Hannerz, U. (1992). *Cultural complexity: Studies in the social organization of meaning.* New York: Columbia University Press.

Harris, M., & Johnson, O. (2007). *Cultural anthropology* (6th ed.). Boston: Allyn & Bacon.

Hemley, R. (2003). *Invented Eden: The elusive, disputed history of the Tasaday.* Lincoln, NE: Bison Books.

Heyes, C. (2018). Identity politics. *Stanford Encyclopedia of Philosophy.* E. N. Zalta (Ed.). https://plato.stanford.edu/archives/spr2018/entries/identity-politics/

Hockett, C. D. (1960). The origin of speech. *Scientific American, 203*(3), 88–96.

Holland, J. H. (1975/1992). *Adaptation in natural and artificial systems*. Cambridge, MA: MIT Press.

James, W. (1880). Great men, great thoughts, and the environment. *Atlantic Monthly, 66*, 441–59.

Johnson, D. W. (1975). Cooperativeness and social perspective taking. *Journal of Personality and Social Psychology, 31*(2), 241–44.

Kahneman, D. (2013). *Thinking fast and slow*. New York: Farrar, Straus and Giroux.

Kakissis, J. (2017, March 18). Israelis and Palestinians "must know how to speak to each other." NPR. Retrieved from http://www.npr.org/2017/03/18/520631310/israelis-and-palestinians-must-know-how-to-speak-to-each-other

Kauffman, S. (1995). *At home in the universe: The search for the laws of self-organization and complexity*. Oxford and New York: Oxford University Press.

King, M. L., Jr. (1963, April 16). Letter from a Birmingham jail [Pamphlet]. Birmingham, AL: American Friends Service Committee.

Klein, R. G., & Edgar, B. (2002). *The dawn of human culture*. New York: Wiley.

LaTour, B. (2005). *Reassembling the social: An introduction to actor-network-theory*. Oxford: Oxford University Press.

Lave, J., & Wenger, E. (1991). *Situated learning: Legitimate peripheral participation*. Cambridge, MA: Cambridge University Press.

Lieberman, P. (1991). *Uniquely human: The evolution of speech, thought, and selfless behavior*. Cambridge, MA: Harvard University Press.

Linton, R. (1937). One hundred percent American. *The American Mercury, 40*, 427–29. Retrieved from https://theamericanmercury.org/2010/07/one-hundred-percent-american/

Lipka, M. (2017, August 9). Muslims and Islam: Key findings in the U.S. and around the world. *FactTank: News in the Numbers*. Pew Research Center. Retrieved from http://www.pewresearch.org/fact-tank/2017/08/09/muslims-and-islam-key-findings-in-the-u-s-and-around-the-world/

Mandelbaum, D. (1958). *Selected writings of Edward Sapir in language, culture, and personality*. Berkeley: University of California Press.

Maslow, A. H. (1943). A theory of human motivation. *Psychological Review, 50*(4), 370–96. doi:10.1037/h0054346

Milgram, S. (1963). Behavioral study of obedience. *Journal of Abnormal and Social Psychology, 67*(4), 371–78.

Milgram, S. (1967, May). The small-world problem. *Psychology Today, 1*(1), 61–67.

Moreno, J. L. (2008). *The essential Moreno: Writings on psychodrama, group method, and spontaneity*. F. Jonathan (Ed.). New Paltz, NY: Tusatala Publishing.

Moskowitz, G. B. (2005). *Social cognition: Understanding self and others*. New York: Guilford Press.

National Academy of Sciences. (2016, November 6–7). Arthur M. Sackler Colloquium: *Extension of Biology through Culture*. Irvine, CA. Retrieved from http://www.nasonline.org/programs/sackler-colloquia/completed_colloquia/Extension_of_Biology_Through_Culture.html

Nunn, C. L. (2000). Collective benefits, free-riders, and male extra-group conflict. In P. M. Kappeler (Ed.), *Primate males* (pp. 192–204). Cambridge: Cambridge University Press.

Polanyi, M. (1958/1962). *Personal knowledge: Towards a post-critical philosophy.* Chicago: University of Chicago Press.

Redfield, R. (1948, November). The art of social science. *American Journal of Sociology, 54*(3), 181–90.

Roan, L., Strong, B., Foss, P., Yager, M., Gehlbach, H., & Metcalf, K. A. (2009, September). *Social perspective taking* (Technical Report 1259). Arlington, VA: U.S. Army Research Institute for the Behavioral and Social Sciences. Retrieved from http://nrs.harvard.edu/urn-3:HUL.InstRepos:4556387

Rogers, E. M. (2010). *Diffusion of innovations.* New York: Free Press.

Ross, L., Amabile, T. M., & Steinmetz, J. L. (1977). Social roles, social control, and biases in social perception processes. *Journal of Personality and Social Psychology, 34*, 485–94. Retrieved from https://www.gwern.net/docs/psychology/1977-ross.pdf

Sherif, M., White, B. J., and Harvey, O. J. (1955). Status in experimentally produced groups. *American Journal of Sociology, 60*, 370–79.

Snyder, M. L., & Frankel, A. (1976). Observer bias: A stringent test of behavior engulfing the field. *Journal of Personality and Social Psychology, 34*(5), 857–64.

Steels, L. (2001). Language games for autonomous robots. *IEEE Intelligent Systems, 16*(5), 16–22. doi: 10.1109/MIS.2001.956077

Steger, M. B. (2003). *Globalization: A very short introduction.* Oxford: Oxford University Press.

Tannen, D. (1990). *You just don't understand: Women and men in conversation.* New York: William Morrow.

Thomas, W. I., & Thomas, D. S. (1928). *The child in America: behavioral problems and programs.* New York: Knopf.

Tomasello, M. (2011, September). Why we cooperate. *Montreal Review.* Retrieved from http://www.themontrealreview.com/2009/Why-we-cooperate-Michael-Tomasello.php

Watts, D. J. (2003). *Six degrees: The science of a connected age.* New York: W.W. Norton.

Whorf, B. L. (1956). Science and linguistics. In J. B. Carroll (Ed.), *Language, thought, and reality: Selected writings of Benjamin Lee Whorf* (pp. 207–19). Cambridge, MA: MIT Press.

Wigginton, N. S. (2016). Evidence of an Anthropocene epoch. *Science, 351*(6269), 134–36.

Wija, Tantri. (2017, February 28). A seat at the (virtual) table. *Santa Fe New Mexican.* Retrieved from http://www.santafenewmexican.com/life/taste/a-seat-at-the-virtual-table/article_a3ea806f-0c13-527d-81b6-a48e5af5e5c6.html

Wimmer, H., & Perner, J. (1983, January). Beliefs about beliefs: Representation and constraining function of wrong beliefs in young children's understanding of deception. *Cognition, 13*(1), 203–28. https://doi.org/10.1016/0010-0277(83)90004-5

Zimbardo, P. (1971, October 25). *The psychological power and pathology of imprisonment.* Statement prepared for the U.S. House of Representatives Committee on the Judiciary, Subcommittee No. 3: Hearings on Prison Reform, San Francisco.

Zimbardo, P. G. (2007). *The Lucifer effect: Understanding how good people turn evil.* New York: Random House.

Zupnik, J. Y. (1995). *Analysis of conflict discourse: Evidence from Israeli-Palestinian "dialogue" events* [Doctoral dissertation]. Boston University.

Index

About the Author

Michael H. Agar received his undergraduate degree from Stanford and his PhD in linguistic anthropology from the University of California, Berkeley. An honorary Woodrow Wilson fellow, NIH Career Award recipient, and former Fulbright senior specialist, he taught at several universities and worked at a number of research institutes over his lifetime. He was named professor emeritus of linguistics and anthropology at the University of Maryland in 1996. For the last decade, until his death in 2017, he worked independently as Ethknoworks, LLC, in Northern New Mexico.